Dear Gayce,

Affectionately, Toots

My Mother's Journal

Live life to the
fullest! Love
is the answer.

Thank you so much
for the beautiful
DVD.

Cheryl Elpers
11/1/2009

Me, Mom, and Dad, 1981

Affectionately, Toots

My Mother's Journal

Cheryl Elferis

Notes From the Journal

We laugh, we cry

We make time fly

Best friends are we

My mother and me.

—Unknown

All farewells should be sudden.

—Byron

This book is dedicated to Nancy "Gammy" Keating.
In her daughter's words,
"She is a mother classy and refined"

Acknowledgments

This project would not have been possible without...

My "Summit" sisters, Marilyn, Keri and Annie, who endured countless readings from drafts of the manuscript over innumerable plates of pasta at Dani's.

My therapist, Susan McConnaughy, who listened to me babble for hours on end, not believing my mother was gone; she helped me make some sense of living in an emotionally chaotic home, coping with a father who no longer recognized me.

My pastor, Jeffrey Nightingale (www.truthforlifecenter.org), who encouraged me to throw out everything I thought I believed and to start over with a new and better perspective.

My editor and writing coach, Judy Gitenstein, who faithfully but gently "cracked the whip" and saw this project to completion.

My husband, Gary, who taught me that a black belt never gives up. I thank you for the care and devotion you showed to my parents, and for the years you stayed home to make Dad's life more enjoyable. My parents would be proud to see the man you've become.

To Edna, My Friend

To Edna, a well-spring of encouragement
She was John's wife, Cheryl's Mom and my Friend;
In each call she made, or note she sent
Her thoughts and words were sincerely meant,
Each kindly adjective was chosen with care
To show her love in word and prayer.
Though her calls and notes were simply external
The cheerful words were truly eternal,
For just as the encourager Barnabas of old
Her messages really touched our soul.
You could never feel depressed or down
When your friend Edna was around
Her friendly smile, each flattering word
She was a humble vessel, used of the Lord!
I'll miss her smile, her words of Love
For now she's smiling from up above,
But one day soon, don't know just when,
With God's leading, we'll meet again!
Yes Edna, my well-spring of encouragement
You were John's wife, Cheryl's Mom and my Friend!

—Iola W. Earl, 2/24/2003

Iola W. Earl was a close friend of my mother, and she gave me this poem just four days after my mother died. —Cheryl

Table of Contents

Introduction

My mother's name is Edna Louise Craig Antonio. This is the only mention of her name that you will see in this book. I refer to her throughout this writing only as "she" or "my mother" or "Toots" (an after-60 nickname), but never by her full name. It is difficult for me to say her name. If I say it out loud or write it, it is an acknowledgment that she is truly gone. I prefer to think of her as having "stepped away temporarily."

This book is a compilation of material taken from two journals, a diary, plus tons of letters and handwritten notes. I never knew about the diary—she kept it before she was married—and I found it while cleaning out her lingerie chest. I gave her the journals on her 78th and 80th birthdays because she had a wonderful way with words and such great stories to tell from her early childhood on. She fascinated young and old alike with her tales of life in New York and Jamaica from the 1930s to the present day. I encouraged her to put those tales in writing, never dreaming that the first journal would culminate in this memoir you read today. I used to question her daily: "Have you written in your journal today?" She never lied to me—she would confess she had been remiss in her duty. Sometimes, for weeks at a time, she wouldn't write anything. I used to threaten her, "If you die before you finish the journal, I will never forgive you." In the letter I tucked into her casket I said that I wasn't angry that she had left us but I was angry that she hadn't finished the

1

journal. It was to be my inheritance, the only thing I had asked her to do for me.

My mother didn't write in chronological order and she seldom used complete sentences. This surprised me because she was such a fanatic about the English language. Huge chunks of her life are missing from the journals. I guess she wrote as the memories came back to her. I think she felt she had plenty of time to go back and fill in the gaps. Since time ran out and her journal was left unfinished, I have attempted to supplement her writings and to talk about the missing years with my version of her life story. For the sake of continuity, I have edited her journal but the diary is word-for-word as she wrote it, with spelling and grammar just as she used it. Much of the material I have added is gleaned from delightful conversations with distant elderly relatives and Mommy's childhood friends, most in their eighties now.

It wasn't until I started doing research for this book that I realized how little I actually knew about my family roots. Every summer visit to Jamaica brought more relatives out of the woodwork; everyone was a "cousin," related somehow. We always visited lots of friends and family when we were in Montego Bay, but I never really knew who was who. Cousin Dorothy illuminated me greatly as to the relations, and without her help, I would not have been able to construct the family tree, sparse as it is. Indeed, she seemed surprised that I not only didn't know who was who, but that I hadn't kept in touch with any of the distant relatives. I hadn't meant to snub anyone; I just never put 2 and 2 together to figure out who they actually were.

This was not an easy project. My emotions swung full circle in putting this memoir together. Reviewing my notes on the bus ride to and from work, I often burst out in spontaneous laughter at some humorous moment recalled.

Other times, reviewing her material, and putting everything down on paper, I cried an awful lot. Indeed, sometimes the loss was so painful that I laid my drafts aside, often for months at a time, and found it difficult to continue. Many times, I felt that the emotions stirred up over poignant memories were too overwhelming and that I would never finish the manuscript. It has taken me five years to complete this book and in some ways, although it is published, it will never really be completed because her legacy continues. It didn't come to an end on February 20, 2003.

In completing this memoir about my mother, by no means do I mean to diminish my father's importance in my life. He was a wonderful father, a man of honor who was always true to his word. If it were not for his spiritual guidance, I am not sure what I would believe in today. And though it was my father's side of the family that I resembled physically and emotionally, it was my mother who shaped my views of the world. He taught me how to pray; she taught me how to cope when prayers seemed unanswered. He reminded me God is love; she reminded me how to demonstrate that love to others. He demonstrated the value of good moral upbringing; she demonstrated the value of inner peace. He took care of all my external needs, and she showed me how to be all that I was meant to be. I am truly blessed to have had both of them influencing me. I could not have chosen or hoped for better parents.

This memoir was a learning experience for me as well. It provided depth to my mother's life and showed me how her earlier experiences shaped the woman she became. I shared in her accomplishments and laughed with her friends. Unfortunately, it also opened my eyes to the emotional pain she experienced in her last years, living with a husband with Alzheimer's.

Affectionately, Toots

For those of you who knew my mother, I hope this brings back fond memories of times shared. To those of you who didn't have the pleasure of my mother's acquaintance, it is my hope that you will get a picture of this grand dame and of the wonderful legacy she left.

Cheryl Craig Antonio-Elferis
July 12, 2009
Toots's 89th birthday

On Mothers and Daughters

Much has been written on the special relationship between daughters and their mothers. Somehow, the umbilical cord between the two is never really severed. Despite circumstances, despite distance and the passage of time, the bond still holds, no matter how tenuous. We may get along, we may argue, we may vow never to speak to each other again, but the cord is still there. We may love each other, we may take each other for granted, we may resent each other, but we're still connected. We may frustrate each other, we may not appreciate each other, we may not understand each other, but we are undeniably linked.

Even if we think we're complete opposites, there is an undercurrent of similarity running through our veins. It might be a look, a spoken word, an attitude, or an emotion—evidence of the cord that binds, despite the outward physical differences. We may have grown up in different eras, we may have worn different clothes, liked different types of men, had different careers or different friends, but we're tethered to each other, whether we like it or not. Spending nine months in her womb has connected us in a way much deeper than the physical. Every woman at some point in her life surely looks in the mirror and sees her mother staring back at her. The seed implanted at conception blossoms into the person we are, but never loses its reflection of the person who birthed it.

In the back of our minds, we just know our mothers will always be there. And when they leave us, whether separated in life or in death, we feel an immeasurable loss. The severing of the cord is painful, more so than we care to admit. For when they die, we feel like a small part of us has been lost as well. Whether our mothers were our heroes or our enemies, we cannot deny their impact on our lives. They helped shape our futures, our personalities, and our dreams.

My mother was an amazing woman. She was strong and courageous, ready to take on the world. At a time when women were just starting to assert themselves in the workplace and society, she galloped through life like a horse with blinders, oblivious to distractions or obstacles. Always conscious of her weak points, she exploited her strengths so that you almost never saw her shortcomings. Was it a façade? Was she really that strong underneath it all? She led a truly blessed life of privilege, growing up in relative wealth, never lacking for anything material. I thought she was invincible.

Mom and me at my aunt Pauline and uncle Locksley's home in Albuquerque, September 1984

It wasn't until she was in her eighties that I saw the enormous effort it took to maintain that aura of strength. And as her strength, physical and mental, slowly ebbed, I got a glimpse of the woman left behind. Although frustrated by emotional and physical pain, she kept her head up high until the end.

Her life summed up: "I have fought a good fight, I have finished my course, I have kept the faith."

The Journal

January 1999

At the presentation of this journal, I quietly debated just how I would frame the following topics. As we age, the mind becomes a well-stocked filing cabinet. "Time" is a river that runs tirelessly into the sea—never backward to the spring.

Valentine's Day 1999

I earnestly decided to attack [the journal] *to review life and add interesting tidbits unblinkingly.*

1920-1925

My mother, Ivy Maud DaCosta, married October 1919 and gave birth to me July 12, 1920 in Manhattan, New York. Both my parents were products of very respected families. My mother (1897-1987) was the daughter of Rachel Johnson and Dr. John DaCosta. My parents had migrated to New York from Jamaica, West Indies in 1918. I was a privileged daughter, idolized by my parents and two precious godmothers, Catherine Henderson and Hytena Dobie and godfather William Dobie. We were all residents of Harlem, which was fast becoming a mecca for Southerners and West Indian migrants— coming north for a better life.

Dad—Egbert C. Craig, proud dad—through all the years regarded me as a special gift and blessing. Mother—very ambitious after giving birth to three children: Edna Louise 1920, Gloria Merle 1923 and Egbert Junior 1926.

Edna Louise Craig, six months old, January 1921

Mom and I became close friends growing up. She took several courses at the Girls' High School—night courses for adults: millinery, English, flower making and dressmaking. Her only means of punishment was chasing Gloria or Junior with a broom—of course, she never caught them. I can never remember a harsh word from Mom.

Affectionately, Toots

The taskmaster and ruler of the clan was Dad. As the U.S. entered the Depression, Dad joined the NYC Board of Education as a custodian engineer. Dad—one of the first men of color to reach Board of Education status. We always had enough—a full, generous life. We saw people standing on [bread] lines and didn't know what they were waiting for. Although others suffered the repercussion of the financial setback, we continued life as usual: piano lessons, ballet lessons, private schools, shopping. There was always food on our table and clothes on our back—we lacked for nothing.

My earliest recollection of life in Harlem was that of enjoying afternoon walks during lovely spring and summer days. I can remember cobblestone streets; I became fearful of the uneven sidewalks not yet asphalted. Although trivial, it was a fear that followed me throughout my entire life.

The Family Tree

It surprised me that Toots, in her writings, referred to her father as Dad because I don't think I ever heard her call him that. Everyone in the family, including her, called him Paubee, pronounced Paw-bee. And, don't ask! No one I've spoken to knows how that nickname came from the full name, Egbert Charles Craig. He was a big man, 6'3" tall. But it wasn't just his height—he was an imposing figure with a bellowing voice and a gentle spirit. He was the first black chief custodian hired by the New York City Board of Education and worked at Junior High School 137 in Manhattan. I can't imagine how much that job paid, but it was apparently enough to maintain a high standard of living for his family. As far as I know, his wife Ivy ("Granny") never worked a day in her life.

Only recently, I learned that Paubee was also an assistant pastor at Refuge Church of Christ, now located at 254 Greene Avenue in Brooklyn. In 2006, I received an invitation in his honor to their 70th Anniversary Celebration—a friends and family reunion. For years, I had driven past Nostrand Avenue on the way home and seen a faded cardboard sign in a third floor window with the words: Elder Egbert Craig. When I asked my mother about the sign, she just shrugged and said she thought it was a church he used to attend. Paubee was a deeply spiritual man and owned the biggest black Bible I have ever seen, even to this day. In the evenings, while I was still straggling at the dinner table, he would come into the kitchen with that Bible. The sound of that Bible thumping down on the table always made me jump. Then he would have a cup of Postum and Pilot crackers while he read the Bible and kept me company. Paubee was the most kind-hearted man I ever knew and I never gave him occasion to discipline me, unlike my cousins who received numerous whippings from him.

Four generations: Mom, Paubee, Granny Queen, and me (Cheryl).
December 1960 in Montego Bay

If Paubee was the patriarch of the Craig clan, surely the matriarch was his mother, whose real name I don't even know. My grandfather always said his mother deserved to be treated like a queen. Those of us who were related called her "Granny Queen" or "Aunt Queen." To everyone else, she was simply "Queen." When I was 16, one of my high school projects involved putting together a family tree. Armed with my cassette tape recorder and notebook, I flew to Jamaica over Easter vacation to interview Granny Queen. I was sure I would be able to complete the entire project with all that she knew. After all, she had been around longer than anybody else in the family.

Granny Queen had failing eyesight with a head of wild white and blond-streaked hair and watery blue eyes, but her mind was sharp as a tack. You could ask her about any family member, any date, any event, and she would be able to recall it with perfect detail. Imagine my disappointment when I sat down with her, turned my tape recorder on, and asked her to relate our family history. She refused, saying there were too many shameful things that should be left unsaid. I knew there were a lot of "relatives" in Jamaica, but she would not answer my questions about exactly how so-and-so was related to us. She would only reinforce what I already knew about our family history, which sadly, wasn't much. Disappointed, I packed up my things and headed back to New York; I never did turn in the project.

Granny Queen was born in 1867 in Jamaica, and that was all I knew about her. There was a rumor circulating in our family, which she would neither deny nor confirm. As the rumor goes, there was a pirate from Scotland named John Craig with whom she had a relationship for many years. My grandfather, Paubee, was the supposed offspring of that relationship. I can find much documentation attesting to pirates in the 1600s and 1700s in Jamaica, but nothing as late as the 1800s or early 1900s. Still, the rumor suited Granny Queen's colorful personality and I could well imagine her dalliance with such a character as John Craig. There was also a rumor about hanky-panky with her sister's husband, but I guess that was part of the shame and scandal she would not talk about, secrets she took to her grave.

Despite her poor eyesight, she enjoyed sharp mental faculties and excellent physical health up until her death at the age of 109. I spent many hours reading the Bible to her and listening to her expound on life and God. Her secret for such a long life was, "Two things: a shot of hot milk and brandy every night before going to bed, and never let me go to the doctor or the hospital –for they will surely kill me." Funny thing—I don't remember her dying, although I know she outlived her only child, Paubee.

When Paubee retired from the Board of Ed, he and Granny packed up their belongings and returned to Jamaica. Paubee had three homes built: two in the town of Montego Bay and one in a suburban development in the hills overlooking MoBay. Granny Queen occupied the 4-bedroom house on 18 Thompson Street. Her care was entrusted to a wonderful woman named Vie DePass, who served Granny Queen faithfully until her death. Miss Vie also doubled as my nanny when I spent summers in Jamaica.

Paubee and Granny moved into the 4-bedroom house around the corner at 17 Tate Street, across the street from Jarrett Park. It wasn't really much of a park, just a large open grassy area with a fenced-in area for sports matches. Occasionally, a cricket match would take place there, and the neighborhood would come alive just for those few days. Raucous stragglers and fans alike would sit on the wooden bleachers, cheering boisterously for the local Jamaican team. On those days, I was warned not to set foot into the park; there were too many shady characters lurking behind the huge, old trees. Those who couldn't afford the entrance fee into the park climbed those old trees lining the perimeter and watched the games from the branches. Once, when I was about 10, I decided I wanted to see what all the whooping and hollering was about. I coerced one of the young maids into escorting me inside the gates during one match, despite her protests and description of what would happen to us if we were ever caught by Granny. She needn't have worried; after half an hour, I was thoroughly bored with the slow-moving game and we sneaked back home. Aside from the infrequent cricket matches, the only thing the park was good for was grazing for the few neighborhood goats. Plus, it provided a shortcut to the church we attended.

The house on Tate Street became a gathering-place for the family, as we all flew in and out of MoBay frequently. Paubee used to say that the Craigs were too big to sit in coach and so we always flew First Class. Of course, in those days, you dressed in your Sunday best to fly. I can clearly remember one such traveling day when I was 5. Just before leaving for the airport, I remember looking down at my white anklets and my black patent leather shoes and saying out loud, "What a lucky little girl I am." In those days, British Airways used to fly non-stop from JFK to MoBay. I was a member of the Junior Jet Club; I had a pin and a little hardcover book. During the flight, a stewardess would escort me to the cockpit and the captain would fill out the logbook with information about the flight. That logbook was one of my prized possessions.

Jamaica

Summers in Jamaica were my happiest childhood remembrances. My favorite memories:

- stealing green almonds from the tree in the vacant lot, hiding them in the broken fire hydrant, and coming back at night, smashing the almonds with a rock and eating the sweet meat inside
- playing jacks for hours upon end with the maids' children
- teaching the girls on the block how to Double Dutch
- taking books out from the local library (the books were all from England and quite different than the ones I was accustomed to)
- squeezing oranges for breakfast—that was the only chore I was allowed to do (I was forbidden to make my bed and my clothes were laid out for me)
- my father teaching me the constellations in the sky and how to tell time and direction by the sun
- buying small bottles of grape juice engraved with drawings of the Flintstones at the only supermarket in town
- being one of the few children on the beach with my own nanny
- sneaking to the Pork Pit with Uncle Junior [Mommy's younger brother] for jerked pork and chicken

Cheryl Elferis

*Me and Mom and my cousin Benita sitting on the steps of my
uncle Louis and aunt Constance's home in Ocho Rios, 1960*

Paubee didn't live long enough to enjoy the retirement he had worked so hard for. He died in 1962, about a year after he retired. It just so happened that he died while Mom and I were visiting one summer. That morning, Paubee and I had been having a race of who could finish their breakfast cereal first. He always let me win. Then, mid-morning, he complained of a pain in his chest and said he was going to lie down. He never got up.

I was outside playing jacks with my best friends—Carmen, a distant "cousin" who lived with us while she attended school and Valerie, who lived

17

next door. One of the maids came out and told us we had to stop playing because Massa Craig had died. I was 5 years old. I didn't know what that meant—that he had died. I couldn't understand what his death had to do with my playing jacks.

I don't remember much of the next few days, except that all my cousins, Aunt Gloria and Uncle Junior started showing up. My cousin Rodney was in the Navy on submarine duty, but he was given leave so that he could attend the funeral. I remember he came to the front gate with his Navy whites and hat still on. Vie stayed home with me while everyone else went to the funeral; I passed the days in complete oblivion.

The death of her father framed my mother's philosophy about enjoying life to its fullest every single day and not putting off the slightest enjoyment. Toots frequently told my dad: "I don't know why you're saving your money. When you die, Cheri and I are going to run through every dime as quick as we can."

Granny—Ivy Maud Craig—was petite and kind-hearted. She was known affectionately as Miss Ivy or Ma Craig. After Paubee passed away, Granny came back to New York to live with us. She was the only grandmother I knew; my father's mother died before I was born. When my parents retired to Jamaica in 1983, they took Granny back to Montego Bay with them and they lived together in the house on Tate Street. Granny passed away in 1987 at the age of 90.

Many years later, cousin Dorothy, who now lives in Spring Valley, New York, helped me connect the dots of the rest of the family tree. As fast as Dorothy could rattle off names, I was writing them down and trying to make the connection between people and faces I hadn't seen for more than 30 years.

I had heard my mother talk about these people all her life; I didn't realize they were actually family.

Dorothy had been born in Jamaica, but came to America at the age of 3. "Auntie Queen" was her mother's aunt; Dorothy couldn't recall her real first name, either. I did find out that Granny Queen was one of the Perry sisters. As a child, we often visited two women whose last names were Perry: Maggie and Daisy. They lived on Dome Street—it wasn't a long walk from our house on Tate Street, but the last stretch was up a very steep and winding hill. We would always be out of breath by the time we finally reached the top.

I had always thought they were two spinster sisters. Now it appears that Maggie had a husband and children and Granny Queen was the third sister. Daisy and Maggie were both thin and spindly and spoke very proper English—the "King's English" we called it. They both suffered from osteoporosis; in those days, it was just called being "hump-backed." My mother used to always say "Stand up straight or you'll end up with a Perry hump."

The Journal: 1925
Brooklyn, New York

My next monumental move—when a 3-family brownstone was purchased from an Italian family who moved to the 200 block of Greene Avenue. Driving in Dad's large black Buick behind a huge truck filled with all the family belongings. Crossing the huge Brooklyn Bridge to our new home in Brooklyn, which ended up being my home for 56 or 57 years—I never moved until my husband, John, retired. Brooklyn was opening up to affluent families, moving up to a still better life. 298 Greene Avenue was a 3-family brownstone—14 rooms on 4 floors. Here was a neighborhood of families of diverse backgrounds—Irish, Jewish, British and a few families of color. Those days, no one dwelled on one's color. We were all Americans. The families on the block were like one big family. Children often ran from house to house, visiting schoolmates.

My parents settled on the Siloam Presbyterian Church on 410 Lafayette Avenue to worship. My parents became members, dragging along their two young daughters, Edna 5 years old and Gloria, 2 years old. We attended the 11:00 a.m. service regularly under Pastor George Shippen Stark. At age 12 (1932), I was confirmed and had my first Communion. I enjoyed being inducted with other youngsters. By then, my sister Gloria was attending St.

Peters Claver Church with stricter guidelines—she always tended to be wayward.

Confirmation, 1932

    I attended a neighboring Public School at age 6 (first grade). Gloria, 3 years my junior, attended the neighborhood Catholic School. She desperately needed firmer supervision than a public school could offer.

    I felt quite grown-up when my parents entrusted me with large amounts of cash as mortgage payments, to be delivered to the former owners (Italians) 2 blocks farther down Greene Avenue, near Nostrand. This went on for years; I was always so very careful not to stop to play with friends along the way. I fulfilled my monthly mission always without incident. Thank God. I would hate to think of the consequences if for any reason I faltered.

I remember beautiful happy childhood days, lacking nothing. I had a frugal but caring mother and a lavish father. We were the first family on the block to own a telephone—Main 2-2165. We were also the first to own a huge black Chevrolet—or was it a Buick? Summers were spent in Meridien, Connecticut with parents of former tenants occupying the street floor (later our kitchen, dining room and den).

298 Greene Avenue

Our home in Brooklyn was a 4-story attached brownstone. When I was a child, it housed 3 generations of Craigs. Paubee and Granny lived on the ground and parlor floors. Mommy's brother, Uncle Junior, and his first wife Gwen lived on the second floor with their two children, Ivy and Billy. And on the top floor were my parents, my older sister Jean, and me.

Mom's sister, Gloria, lived not far away on Macon Street with her two youngest children, Arnold and Barbara ("Peewee"). Her two oldest children, Sondra and Rodney, lived at 298, having been formally adopted by Paubee and Granny.

I was the youngest child in the house, and my older cousins bristled when I was entrusted to their care. Granny insisted they take me with them whenever they went out. I am sure that was a major cramp in their teen-age lifestyle; they were older by 10 years, at the least. However, my cousins soon discovered a practical solution to the problem. On the ground floor, we had a huge walk-in linen closet lined with wooden shelves. My cousins would tell me that we were going to play a game of hide-and-seek. Then one of them would tell me to hide in the linen closet. I would pull a blanket down from one of the shelves, make myself comfortable, and sit in that closet for hours, satisfied that I had the best hiding place and that nobody was sure to find me. When they returned, they would "pretend" to find me and the game would be over. None of the adults was ever the wiser for their prank and I was never missed. I thought it was the greatest game. To this day, I am completely comfortable in total darkness.

When Paubee and Granny returned to Jamaica, we moved down to the two lower floors. My parents lived there until 1983, when they sold the house and retired to Montego Bay.

Thanksgiving 1959 at Greene Avenue.
Aunt Vera, Uncle Vivian (Dad's brother), me and Mom

Many of my fondest childhood memories at 298 revolved around food. The Craigs were all people of large stature—all the males over 6 feet, and none of the women shorter than 5'10." I can remember Paubee saying, "A full stomach is the best sign of prosperity." We weren't a large family, but when we got together—Thanksgiving at 298, Christmas at Aunt Gloria's—they were very special occasions indeed. I was always amazed at the amount of food we could put away. The concept of "Thanksgiving leftovers" was a foreign phrase. There never were any leftovers.

My mother always said, "You must live to eat, not eat to live." She wasn't fond of cooking, although she cooked every night. She did enjoy baking. All the neighbors were recipients of a constant flow of cakes and cookies. In her later years, her cookies were hard as rocks or burnt to a crisp. Nevertheless, she continued to bake and give them away, much to my dismay. I have to give Dad credit, though. He ate those cookies like a champ and never once complained. I imagine most neighbors graciously accepted them and then pawned them off on a family pet.

If Mom had her way, we would have eaten out every night. Our favorite restaurant was Candlelight in Brooklyn Heights. It seems like we were there every Saturday night. I was a picky eater as a child ("You didn't get that from the Craig side of the family"), and I always ordered the same thing— Salisbury steak—fancy words for a hamburger. I loved that restaurant. Mom taught me that you must be willing to try new foods, eat slowly, and savor every bite. A meal was not merely nourishment for the body, it was meant to be an experience. Nothing dismayed her more than my father wolfing down his meal without ooh-ing and aah-ing over every mouthful. He "ate to live," sadly.

When they moved back to New York in the '80s, Mom discovered two new concepts in eating—take-out and restaurant buffets. She was like a kid in a candy shop at salad and buffet bars, often to my father's embarrassment. He would cringe at every trip to refill her plate while I would cheer her on. "You only live once" was her justification. And heaven help my father if he tried to rush her. The more he would say, "Come on, come on, hurry up," the slower she would eat. I came to view mealtimes as sources of entertainment, as the interactions between my parents, particularly in public, never failed to amuse me.

Toots collected thousands of recipes—purely for the art of collecting, not that she ever had any intention of actually trying to cook anything. I found lots of recipes, all in her own handwriting that I wish she had tried, like sweet potato fritters, as well as others, such as lasagna, that I wish she hadn't. She made Dad crazy watching the Food Channel on TV. She would call me at work to find a recipe on the Internet that she had just seen on some cooking show. She just had to have it—not that she ever planned to make the dish.

She liked a few things that I could cook, like omelets, corn muffins and sweet pickle relish.

Everyone has favorite recipes that only their mother could make in her own special way—our comfort foods. I would be a millionaire if I had a dollar for every time I said to my mother: "After you go, I'll never eat such-and-such again." Some recipes just can't be reproduced. My mother always estimated on her measurements, something I also do, much to the chagrin of friends who want any of my recipes. Sometimes I think it's the pot or pan that makes the difference. Nothing can replace those heavy cast-iron skillets; I still use my grandmother's to sear London broil.

I'll miss her rice and peas. I can never get my rice dry enough. Dad disdained pork—he would have had a stroke on the spot if he ever knew that she used bacon grease as the base. I never ate the peas (actually red kidney beans), but it's not rice and peas without them.

I guess I won't be eating oxtail either: sweet meat so tender it fell off the bone, in a starchy brown gravy. Or beef tongue, a delicacy that has to be cooked just right.

No more fried dumplings—great for breakfast with strawberry jam. How did she get them so brown and crisp on the outside and still soft inside? I always end up with raw dough in the middle. Too much handling, she would say.

No more fried liver and onions, a favorite Sunday morning breakfast special. The meat was so tender you didn't need a knife to cut it.

No more banana fritters. Just the other day, we had a bunch of overripe bananas and I just stood there looking at them, realizing I didn't have a clue how to make the fritters. I would have loved some fritters, drenched with pancake syrup. We ended up throwing the bananas away.

Unfortunately, Mom wasn't big on self-control. Tastes were to be indulged, even if it included eating forbidden foods. As a result, she struggled with her weight her entire life, finally resigning herself to the fact that she would always be big. Diabetes or no diabetes, she could easily put away a half-gallon of ice cream. Sad to say, I have inherited those yearnings and have absolutely no self-control when it comes to food.

The Journal: 1932

Graduation from Public School 45 was a highlight for the entire family. During the last grade (eighth), girls were required to attend sewing and cooking classes. We each made our own graduation dresses, all by hand. It was fun stitching every seam, until the last stitch revealed a dusty-white graduation dress—dusty from each week's handling so many times—reopening seams and re-sewing. Finally, Graduation day arrived with all its fanfare. It was a happy, fulfilling experience having completed public school. I was looking forward to attending high school (Girls High School at Nostrand and Halsey Streets).

After one semester at Girls High, my parents decided I would be better off elsewhere. I am not sure whose brilliant idea it was; it does, upon reflection, sound like my Dad's idea. He later said that he wanted his two girls trained as "ladies." He was a very strong man physically and mentally. Only the best for his girls. So, plans were begun to ship both daughters off to finishing school for ladies.

The Journal: 1933

By age 13, I was a well-read piano student. I became the pianist for the Sunday School. The following year, the church organist, Mr. Hugo Bourne, fell ill. I was asked to try to play the pipe organ during his illness. Mr. Bourne retired, confident that I could serve until a replacement could be found. I was always very proficient at sight-reading and could play any hymn selected. For 6-8 months, I filled in until a more accomplished organist, Mrs. Clarissa Saunders Samarian, was found. I was to be her assistant until I left the country for private boarding school. I also joined the choir as an active member. When Mrs. Samarian left, I was again called to fill in. Not long after, Mrs. Florence Mills became senior organist. I was always on-call until 1934, when my parents decided to send me to Westwood [a boarding school in Jamaica]. *I really enjoyed these years, too young to experience bouts of nerves. Thank God I survived this period. I always did my very best with God's help. I was mature enough to pass as an adult.*

I returned to Siloam in March 1938. The church outgrew its present quarters at 404-410 Lafayette. There was a migration of influential members moving to the Park Slope section where many of "Brooklyn's 400's" now lived in spacious brownstone buildings. When the church moved to 260 Jefferson, I resumed my position of assistant organist. I was then attending the Brooklyn Conservatory of Music, where I performed several concerts and received a diploma. With the pending marriage, plus classes at Brooklyn College, my workload became burdensome, in addition to teaching at home some evenings and all day Saturdays. At age 18, I was still quite active at Siloam.

The Journal: 1934-1938
Years at Westwood

With the house at 298 Greene Avenue fully paid for, my parents were focusing on sending their daughters to Montego Bay to enjoy the luxury of a British education (Jamaica was then a British colony). I was registered to attend Westwood, a High School for Ladies, and Gloria would go to Mount Alvernia—both in Jamaica, West Indies. We three traveled by ship with a mutual friend of the family and her young son. It was quite an elegant journey—dressing up for dinner aboard the ship. I don't quite remember how long the ship took to reach Jamaica.

The ship landed at Kingston with two nervous American girls, with our steamer trunks filled with linens, school uniforms, bedding, towels, bath essentials—all labeled with printed name labels. How my mother ever achieved this gigantic task—preparing two daughters for such a trip (without a murmur) was unbelievable. But we were fully prepared for the trip. I can't quite remember month or the exact year (1933-1934). We were both deposited with a spinster "maternity-nurse" who delivered babies of wealthy Syrian families at home.

This was quite an experience for us as Americans. I was looked on in awe by adults and children alike—they envied us as native New Yorkers—a place they had only read about in school. Anywhere we went, we were stared at, like something exotic. We were often questioned by adults in fascination. Two days later, a "mistress," as the staff members were called, came by bus to Nurse Euphemia, 18 Spanish Town Road, to transport me the following day by bus to Westwood High School for Girls (located in Stewart Town, Trelawny, Jamaica).

Westwood was a religious private boarding school for young ladies. One had to be the children of professional parents. We were a real privileged class of girls. Because I was the only American, I was looked upon as a rare specimen. I can recall the other girls snickering and whispering as I entered the dormitory. I was later told that, prior to my arrival, the headmistress, Miss Mae Jeffrey-Smith, warned the girls of a new arrival from America and that they should be on their best behavior to welcome me. I was shown to my room—a bed and a closet with a cretonne covering. No doors—no locks. As I went about opening my suitcases, laying out my linens in the closet—in post haste, I had a crowd surrounding me. They were amazed—silk colored undies, bras, panties and slips. Under close scrutiny, one first then the others picked up pieces of my personal articles—oohing and aahing. Only one girl in the group came to my rescue; we are close friends to this day. She urged them to leave me alone. It was quite scary—all those natives—eyeing a newcomer.

Month after month passed with gradual disappearance of any article of clothing I left on outside lines to dry. There were such strict rules at the school. The standards were so high. Yet, I was the constant victim of petty theft. I think the other girls were just jealous and being spiteful.

The school itself was very primitive. The bathrooms were outside, along with rows of showers. Schedules of daily duties were posted on each dormitory door, including the list of daily showers. My dorm housed girls 12-

13 years of age. Gongs and bells were used throughout the premises to announce wake-up calls and activities. The dining room was also primitive— no electricity, only kerosene lamps. Of course, there was no running water except for the outdoor facilities.

*This photo was taken at Easter time, at Westwood,
a private girls' boarding school in Jamaica, 1935*

It was not easy. I was scared most of the time, for fear these wild natives would one day turn entirely against me. My dad was very, very generous. Packages of new black silk stockings with gold stripes arrived every month.

Silk—this is long before nylon. And huge boxes of candies would arrive for me. All mail was given to the Headmistress who opened all packages before calling me to the office to receive them.

I am forced to stray here to remark "why" until today I write so many letters. Most of the students were natives of Jamaica. I was at that time the only American. In addition to the correspondence I received from my Brooklyn friends, my dad showered me with 3-4 letters each week. I was always receiving mail, while witnessing firsthand the disappointment on the faces of the other girls just longing for a letter from anyone, which seldom happened. This bothered me. To somehow atone for my good fortune, I shared every package I received. The pilfering tapered off. But there was always something missing, either from my dormitory closet or classroom desk.

All letters written by students to family were read and censored by the prefect, so there was never an opportunity to complain to parents regarding food, services, etc. Westwood served several West Indian dishes. I just could not develop a taste for so many foreign dishes, so I refused dinner several times. I seldom had a full meal. Back in my dormitory, I would nibble on cookies sent by my dad. I was smart enough to secure a tight stash in my closet.

Each day's schedule was quite rigid and supervised by a teacher:

> *5 am: shower*
>
> *6 am: morning tea*
>
> *7 am: morning worship assembly*
>
> *8 am: classes begin*
>
> *10 am: breakfast—a full meal—rice and peas, squash, pumpkin and canned sardines or beef stew*

I can't quite recall afternoon schedules, except for more classes.

6 pm: supper—1 slice of hard dough bread with butter and hot chocolate. Unpasteurized milk with the fat swimming on top.

I might add, during the 3 ½ years I spent there, including holidays in Kingston, I was never offered one egg. Miss Reside from Ireland was the only instructor who enjoyed one egg and thinly sliced toast. How I wished I had just one egg! I made up for this on holidays. There were several times during outdoor study period, I would see a student opening a can of condensed milk, pour some on dry crackers and give the impression she was in heaven (so hungry were we all). I just could not join them, politely declining with "No thank you." That was the one feature that saved me; I was never termed a "stuck-up" which could have been devastating. Only God knows what the reaction would be. Perhaps it was because I was always ready to share my bounties from America.

At Westwood, I continued my music (piano) studies, sitting favorable for each yearly examination under the Royal School of Music London, from which I hold several diplomas. Examiners would come to Jamaica each year to test students and the diplomas were issued from London.

I truly missed my Mom and Dad. I saw my sister only during vacations. Gloria attended Mount Alvernia, a Catholic boarding school some distance away. On one vacation break, I joined my mother in Kingston. Her first reaction was shock when she saw how thin I was. Then she heard me burp and decided I was not eating well. Too much gas build-up. That was it. "You are not going back!" Without ever returning for my belongings—clothes, trunk, tennis racket and balls—nothing was retrieved. I do not know up to this day how my mother pulled this coup without Dad's say-so. My dad was the boss of the family in a soberly, respectable manner. But it was effective—not another word of Westwood. I was certainly happy to close this chapter of my life and I thank my mom for her bravery in pulling this off.

2009: A Bit More About Westwood High School

In 1812, Stewart Town was established in the parish of Trelawny in Jamaica. The land was very fertile and it became an ideal place for coffee plantations. There were several churches in the town, including an Episcopal, Methodist and a Baptist church. In the late 1800s, the pastor of the Baptist church, Rev. William Menzie Webb, visited England and was the guest of Dr. Frederick Trestrail of Bristol, a former Secretary of the Baptist Missionary Society. When asked by Mrs. Trestrail what he considered the greatest need in Jamaica, Rev. Webb replied, "A High School for the training of native girls along with others regardless of class or colour." Mrs. Trestrail presented the idea to other ladies, rallied support and provided Rev. Webb for the funding of his dream. In 1880, the school began under the name of The Manchester Girls' School, but soon rapidly outgrew the building. In 1880, nine acres of land were purchased and buildings erected for a new school. The name was changed to Westwood High School. Teachers came from England and the school continued to prosper. By 1913, the school was self-supporting. Since then, the school continued to prosper, charging moderate fees for tuition as well as receiving Government grants.

To this day, Westwood is a thriving pillar of education in Stewart, Jamaica. I contacted the school in an effort to gain access to their archives. Unfortunately, most of their records were destroyed in the terrible hurricane of 1991. The friend Mom mentioned who came to her rescue was Myrtle Freeman, who we visited often in Manhattan during the '80s and '90s. She passed away several years ago so I was unable to interview her. I've also lost contact with her daughter, who I always looked up to and admired for her "wild streak," as Toots called it.

There were other friends that Mom met at school that she ran into later in life, such as Myrtle. Mom wasn't close to Myrtle while attending Westwood. They didn't become friends until after they were both married and living in New York. One day, Myrtle walked into the YWCA to sign up for swimming lessons. When she saw Mom, Myrtle said, "I know you—Don't you remember, Edna? We went to school together." Since then, the women kept in touch. When Myrtle and her husband Bruce had their first baby in April of 1950, my mother called her and said, "I know that baby keeps you up at night. John and I will come over and baby-sit while you two go to a movie." At the time, my mother was pregnant herself with Jean. Giving birth within months of each other created a special bond between the two friends.

Phyllis was another friend of my mother's from Westwood. She was already attending the school when Mom started, and was, like the other students, fascinated with the idea that she was a foreigner. Her memories of my mom: she was so musical, so charming, a beautiful person.

The Journal: 1938

In February, Gloria and I were scheduled to return home—Hallelujah! We were spending the last few weeks with a relative of my mother in Montego Bay. EXCEPT—in December 1937, a cousin, Dorrell Buddle, asked if I would mind accompanying him to visit his good friend John, who was recently wounded in a car accident. It was night; however, I felt safe with Dorrell and said "yes." The hospital was poorly lit. However, Dorrell found the way— with me in tow—to a bed with someone with a bandaged face. This was my very first visit—EVER—to a hospital. No introduction was made. I felt queasy, but my heart went out the injured young man. That was that.

Three weeks later, Dorrell brought the young man, fully recovered, to meet me. There was a bond that first visit. We went for walks along the beach (well lit). I had no qualms about going alone, unescorted. Somehow, I felt safe with him. Something clicked between us immediately. It seemed to be "love at first sight." The spark grew stronger each week. We then realized we had little time to really know each other. All he knew was that I was from America. After a few chaperoned dates to the beach, we both realized this was something very special. The eve of my sailing, he and Dorrell drove my sister and I from Montego Bay to Kingston for our departure (March 8th, I think). That last day aboard the ship was so very sad. The parting—amidst friend and guardian, Dorrell—was very subdued. We lingered over the last kiss and finally separated. For the next six years, we corresponded by mail only, getting to know each other—our likes, our goals and future plans.

John Andrew Durrell Antonio. Portrait taken in Jamaica, 1936, when he was 20 years old

When I returned home from Westwood, my parents decided that I would continue my musical studies with the Brooklyn Conservatory. Here, I excelled and enjoyed the challenges of each examination. At the same time, I registered at Brooklyn College and attended evening classes.

Cheryl Elferis

One of my friends urged me to seek employment. Apparently, all my peers were gainfully employed under the government NYA (National Youth Administration). With my musical background, I was offered two positions: teaching at the downtown Glee Club or the YWCA. My mother decided I'd meet a better class of ladies at the YWCA. So at age 18, I started work at the Brooklyn YWCA at 221 Ashland Place, the "colored branch," at a salary of $25 per month. Living at home, with no expenses, I felt rich. I offered my parents my first paycheck. My dad became furious. I received the brunt of his anger; he accused me of becoming a woman. It was difficult calming him down. It was his "awakening call"—I was no longer his little girl.

After two years, the Ashland Place building was demolished. I was one of only two staff members who were asked to join the Brooklyn Central Branch at 30 Third Avenue. I enjoyed working there several years as I climbed the business ladder with compensating salaries. I soon became Director of Room Registry, then on to Assistant Director of Membership. It was fun and really enjoyable work.

I can vividly recall sitting at the front desk as Miss Elizabeth DeMaris congratulated me on my 25th birthday. I felt so grown up. I soon gained favor with each elegant Brooklyn Heights staff and board members, and attended weekend meetings at their country estates. There was never any suggestion of discrimination—never, ever. I remained in the employ of the YWCA for 25 years. I enjoyed every day—hardly like work—terrific ladies. I grew up becoming quite the lady—paying strict attention to manners and dress codes—always with my hat and gloves.

What beautiful years! Between duties at the YWCA and music club Mu-Te-Or (an organization of musicians, organists and teachers). I had also

41

taken to teaching piano lessons at home on Saturday—all day 7:30 am until 5:30 pm. After a number of years, I began to feel too fatigued with the hectic schedule. Enjoying each activity, I had always seemed to have a resilient attitude. I decided to forego college for a while (a mistake—Yes? No?). I ended my studies with the Brooklyn Conservatory shortly after I wed. I decided years later to pursue my Bachelors Degree in Music by mail. I found this quite gratifying.

Mom and YWCA friend, Gertrude Hergot, Brooklyn, New York, 1944

I should here state that my Dad was so disappointed that I did not take advantage of his offer to further my music studies in London. He was so proud of my musical achievements. My dad was a perfectionist, always aiming high in all respects. He was a dedicated father and such an inspiration to so many. This reminds me of a friend I met through another friend. She exclaimed that when she heard that I was visiting in Mandeville, Jamaica, she had to meet me to say," If it were not for your Dad, my sister Lily Dunn and I would never have become what we are today. Because of your father—your Dad put my sister and me through Teacher's College in Mandeville." I was quite surprised to hear this. I thanked her and promised to stay in touch with her. She was most gracious.

My dad was quite a philanthropist, known for his generosity, first with his family and others in need. He was an excellent supporter and generously so. When I returned to New York in 1938, a Wissner baby grand piano awaited me. It was hand-made, the last made by Mr. Wissner himself. To this date, I cherish this piano. Dad was never a showy person—all his generosity was done quietly. His mother has always been his Queen—and lived as a queen to her dying day, July 4, 1976 at age 109. I could write a chapter just on my parents. Fortunately, they both loved my John. Life can truly be so beautiful— my testimony to a life of so much joy and love.

My Mother's "Animals"

My mother had a cape of stone martens. They were the pelts of little animals that looked like foxes, complete with beady glass eyes and dangling paws with long curved claws. The pelts were arranged so that the jaw of one was sewn shut holding on the rear end of the pelt next to it. The "animals" always went to church on Sunday morning. Occasionally, the "animals" made an appearance at other cultural events, but only when we traveled by car. As far as I can recall, the "animals" didn't take public transportation.

At church, kids used to vie for seats in the pew behind my mother. They would spend the greater part of the service daring each other to touch the "animals."

Right now, the "animals" are sitting on the top shelf of my closet. What can I possibly do with them? Who would ever want them, much less actually wear them in public?

Musical Talent

My mother was an extremely accomplished classical pianist. The Wissner baby grand was her 18th birthday present from her father. On the Saturdays when she taught lessons, there was a steady stream of children who played upstairs with me while waiting their turn for their lesson. A one-hour music lesson was $3.00. My father actually paid my mother for my lessons.

Over the years, dozens of children became skilled pianists under my mother's tutelage. I, alas, was not one of them. I inherited none of my mother's skill or musical talent—only a passion that more often than not ended up in utter frustration. When my mother played the piano, it got up and danced around the room. As soon as I touched the keyboard, I swear I heard it groan in anticipated despair. Mom would push me to practice more— promising that if I persisted, I too could coax magic from the ivory keys. It never happened.

In a last desperate attempt, my mother selected Lost Happiness from Felix Mendelssohn's "Songs Without Words for the Piano." It was the most moving and beautiful piano work I have ever heard, even to this day. I was determined to master it and I practiced and practiced and practiced—to no avail. Eventually, I gave up trying and resigned myself to the fact that I would never play it like she did.

Shortly afterward, I came to believe that my musical ineptitude might extend only to the piano and that because I truly enjoyed music, perhaps I could master another instrument. At age 13, I informed Toots that I wanted to play the guitar. Off we went to Sam Ash, where we bought a guitar and a how-to book. I think the guitar cost $15.00. I tried to play it two or three times, after which its only purpose in my room was to collect dust. I actually hid it under my bed hoping my mother wouldn't see it and ask me how I was coming along with my practice. I needn't have worried—not once did she ask my how I was doing with my guitar lessons.

A year later, I asked her for a violin, thinking I would do better on that instrument. Instead, she bought me a beautiful purple enamel violin pin, which I wear and treasure to this day. She said nothing when she handed me the box. She didn't have to. I knew this was her way of saying she wasn't going to buy me any more instruments. I don't think we ever discussed my musical ability—or lack of it—ever again.

Music was her passion and she could be moved to tears at a good piano recital. She was always the first to stand and shout "Bravo" at the end of a particularly inspiring concert, a practice that always embarrassed me as a child. I used to shrink down in my seat hoping no one would notice I was with this crazy woman. Never mind that other people were also standing and clapping. Why did she always have to be the first one?

The only time I didn't mind standing was during the Hallelujah Chorus of Handel's Messiah. Handel first performed the cantata in front of King George. When the Hallelujah Chorus was played, the King was so moved he stood to his feet. And when the king stands, everyone stands. Thus started the tradition of standing during the playing of that chorus at any performance. When I was a child, it seemed everyone knew this and stood, even without prompting from the conductor, whose duty it is to ensure that everyone respects this tradition. However, it seems that this tradition is no longer upheld. Perhaps people just don't know. Perhaps conductors have become lazy. My mother was always horrified at conductors who failed to instruct the audience to stand. She considered them ignorant and refused to attend any of their concerts.

A sheet from Mom's notebook on musical composition

I knew she had studied music formally but I didn't realize the extent of her training until I found her diploma from a correspondence course she took from the Royal Conservatory of Music, London. I found pages and pages of her exams and notes. I didn't know musical studies could be so complicated. I learned scales and keys, but that was nothing compared to her courses. One course was entitled History, Analysis and Appreciation of Music. I didn't even understand the questions: Characteristics of German art songs. Composers of Chorlied music. Importance of the firm Ballard. Pairs of voices. Terms I had never heard.

One of the questions on the exam I found particularly interesting: Is music able to express something beyond the mere sound? Had you ever heard her play, you would know the answer. I guess that's why it bothers me that I can no longer "hear" her music in my head. I used to be able to sight-read a classical piece and hear her playing. I seem to have lost that ability.

In her 50s, Mom decided that she wanted to study jazz. She signed up for piano lessons at a studio in Manhattan—I think I went with her once. But she was so accustomed to playing classical music that she found the transition difficult and soon stopped the lessons.

Mom did her own practicing at least one hour each day. Sometimes, when I came home from school, I would tiptoe quietly into the dining room so as not to disturb her. I would sit and do my homework while she played, her fingers flying effortlessly over the keys. Although she hardly acknowledged my presence in the room, when she knew I was there, she always ended her practice with "Lost Happiness," knowing that it was my favorite. She renamed it "Cheryl's Song."

From then on, at every recital and performance, she always included "Cheryl's Song" in her repertoire.

I have very few regrets in life; but one is that I never made a recording of my mother playing this piece. It has unfortunately lived up to its name and become a "Lost Happiness" for me.

Formal portrait before a piano recital. Brooklyn, 1938

Achievement

Toots was one of the first feminists. Not the bra-burning, men-hating kind. Rather, she was of the "You can be anything you want to be" mindset. When other little girls my age were wearing frilly pink dresses and dreaming of being a nurse or teacher, I was running around in jeans and T-shirts, thinking if I could imagine it—I could do it. In school, my mother considered cooking and typing classes a waste of time—"You can always learn those things later." Throughout high school and even college, I must have changed my mind a hundred times about what I wanted to be. But no matter what the "occupation of the day" I was entertaining at the time, she always just said, "Okay." On only one occasion when I said I wanted to be a ballerina, did she try to dissuade me, saying that I was not graceful enough.

Mom didn't believe in glass ceilings. There was no limit to what one could accomplish. On the other hand, there were no excuses. She was horrified at the thought that people might use discrimination as a reason for failure, claiming you could always rise above your circumstances. Using a reason such as growing up poor or being of a minority race to justify one's lack of accomplishment just didn't fly with my mother and her circle of friends. The greater the obstacles you had to overcome, the stronger your character would develop. Gender was the least acceptable excuse for failure. She encouraged me to be an astronaut when I first expressed an interest in the stars. When I was seven, I remember her telling me I should aspire to be

President of the United States. Just President—not first female President. People were supposed to be judged for what they did, not whether they were male or female, black or white. Here I should correct myself—my mother never uttered the word "black" in reference to someone. "Colored" was the politically correct term at the time.

Failure of any kind was not tolerated. Although I am lazy by nature (a trait directly inherited from my mother—nobody eats and sleeps like a Craig), both my parents pushed me to be an A student. My formal lessons started when I was three. With Mom working the evening shift at the YWCA, Dad was entrusted with my care from 5 p.m. to 9 p.m. After dinner, to keep me occupied and out of his hair, he would give me books to read. The books were school primers from Jamaica. Each page had pictures and the name of the object under the picture. Why they didn't use those books in the New York City school system was beyond me. A chimpanzee could have learned to read with those books.

By the age of 5, I was a proficient reader. In kindergarten, I wrote the principal of the school, P.S. 270, a note (which I still have to this day) explaining that I was bored. The children were learning their ABCs and about Abraham Lincoln and I was anxious to learn more. I signed my mother's name on to the note and took it into the principal's office.

The next day, the principal, Mr. Marcy Cowan, called my mother and me in to discuss the note, not believing that I could possibly think myself too advanced for kindergarten. Mom picked up the Sports section of the New York Times that was on the principal's desk, handed it to me and told me to start reading out loud. I read it flawlessly, much to his amazement. The next day, I found myself in second grade, but because I was only five, I stayed only half a day. At the time, my mother worked in the school library and taught music appreciation. So, after lunch, instead of going back to class, I would go up to the library and wait for her, devouring every book I could get my hands on. Two months later, I was transferred to another public school that had classes for Intellectually Gifted Children. There, I was challenged with advanced classes and really learned to enjoy school. Special classes included Roman and Greek mythology as well as Latin, which helped me greatly with English and other foreign languages.

This picture was taken in 1962 when my mother was school librarian and music appreciation teacher at P.S. 270 in Brooklyn

While other children had to bring in extra money (2 cents for milk, 1 cent for a pretzel), I "earned" my snacks every day by winning the spelling bee in class every single day. Unfortunately, the part of my brain that had to process mathematical skills proved to be seriously deficient. If I stared at a page with numbers on it, eventually the numbers would stand up, walk to the edge of the paper and roll off the paper on to the floor. I can remember being 9 and still having difficulty telling time on a clock. My knees would weaken whenever my father would ask me to recite the times table. The fact that he could do complex math problems in his head didn't help my cause. He couldn't understand how I could be so bright but not be able to do 7 x 4.

In grade school, I learned to fear for my life if I came home with anything less than an A on a test or a report card. So, by the third grade, I perfected the art of forgery and signed my parents' name on any "less-than-acceptable" graded homework assignments and tests. Sometimes, for months, I wouldn't bring any report cards home. My parents never asked how I was doing in school; they just assumed I was getting straight As. The forgeries continued until the ninth grade, when a D in math forced me finally to confess.

I had gone from public junior high school to St. Angela Hall Academy for Christian Young Women in Brooklyn, and found myself academically way behind my classmates, particularly in math. Actually, I failed the algebra course that first year. I don't know what made me think I might possibly have passed—I never scored any higher than a 20 on any test that year. Some tests, I got all the questions wrong. And I had done one of the girl's French homework all year in exchange for her doing my math homework. So, at the end of the year, when I got an F, I should not have been surprised. However, I flung myself at the Sister's feet, begging for mercy. I told the Sister that if she gave me an F, I would have to run away from home that very evening, rather than face my parents. She must have believed me, because she changed the grade to a D, which was bad enough, but the best I could hope for. At the dinner table that evening, unable to force any food down because I felt like I was going to die, I told my parents about the D in math. Mom never even blinked, just kept right on eating, but Dad was furious. He ranted and raved and threatened to come to the school the next day. I pleaded and begged with him not to, fearful that the nun would tell him my grade really should have been an F. Somehow, he calmed down and thankfully, nothing more was said about the grade.

That didn't stop me from bribing my classmates to do my math homework and yes, even giving me the answers on math tests throughout high school. In exchange, I did their French and English homework. We justified ourselves by rationalizing that French was as useless to them as math was to me. Even in college, I tried to get through statistics by promising to work for the professor for free if he would just give me a passing grade without having to take any tests. I wasn't being dishonest, just desperate. To this day, I detest anything to do with math.

Toots believed that if you put your mind to it, you could overcome any handicap and achieve anything you wanted. Just because something was difficult was not reason not to do it, and do it well. From her encouragement, I developed my work ethic—"Do what you have to do"—a phrase anyone who has ever worked with me has heard a thousand times. She taught me that if you attempt to hurdle a mountain on your first try, then you probably were setting yourself up for failure. But if you set goals and raised the bar just a little each time, then you could measure your accomplishments, no matter how small, and that would be enough to inspire you to go on.

The Journal: June 1944

While out to lunch at the YWCA, a telephone call came through the switchboard from Penn Station from John Antonio. My co-worker, Mrs. Gertrude Hergot, took the message. As I returned from lunch, "Gert" said excitedly, "Your John is at Penn Station waiting for you." He had joined a group of Jamaicans that came to the USA as part of a government farm group. They were scheduled to leave New York with no details. I dashed like mad to Penn Station. Frantically, I located the platform and found my John— amazing! I flew into his arms exhilarated, so happy I caught him before his train left for Michigan. We enjoyed about 15-20 minutes together before we parted and his train left. I really can't explain how I ever made it back to the YWCA in Brooklyn, too hepped up to work. I was given the afternoon off to go home to ponder! My mother shared my enthusiasm. This was the beginning of a long-term romance based on respectability and love.

As soon as John became settled in his new home (Saginaw, Michigan), plans were made for me to visit him. My childhood insurance plan, Metropolitan Life, was due to mature soon. I can still vividly remember the agent visiting each month to collect weekly fees—10 cents per week per child.

To my surprise, my mother handed me $500 and said, "Go to your John." I was stunned. Other than Westwood, I had never ventured too far from home alone—unescorted. Then, this! I could not believe my ears. Strange enough, *no word on this subject came from my Dad, who was the authoritarian of the family. His word was law. Candidly, I am sure my mother had his full cooperation. My dad was very strict with his two girls. Absolutely no young men came to call. Young men, mostly from Siloam Church, were allowed to look (what we used to term a "come-hither interested" look), but nothing further ("tee hee").*

Brooklyn, 1947. My mother always wore suits

Startling! How did my parents ever come to reason, allowing their first-born to go to Michigan unescorted?? Could it be they had faith in me to uphold my training as a lady?? Thank God. It was music to my ears. After six years relationship by mail (1938-1944), I would meet John in Saginaw. We had fun together reliving so many lonely hours.

The Diary: 1944

Wednesday, July 5: Left NY for Saginaw, Michigan. A second later would have missed train. Arrived in Detroit 7:30 am next morn. Took taxi to 998 Mack Street. Met Luxemburg fellow (music lover) and had a grand time on the train.

Thursday: Left Detroit for Saginaw YWCA. Miss Nichols showed me to room. Rest all PM. Went to show at nite—saw Sherlock Holmes "Scarlet Claw and Saint."

Friday: Rest again. The usual routine. Couldn't eat any food—drank 8 bottles of Coke all day.

Saturday: Honey called me at 8:30 am. Was cheering to hear his voice. Came to see me and we spent day together. Breakfast at Home Dairy—went to park and lunched—looked for (???) and ended back at the park, the only place we knew. Honey's really fine—perfect gentleman. Left me at 1:00 am.

Sunday: Honey called me 10 am. Breakfast—practiced (piano)—went to sleep. Dined out—went to service at Salvation Army—attracted by "He Lives." Spent rest of eve writing letters.

Monday: Stayed in bed until 1 pm. Brunched at 2 pm. Mailed sugar and tea to Honey. Practiced. Miss home. Honey called 8:30 pm—plans to spend a few days with me.

Tuesday—Je leve a la neuve heures. Waited for Honey at Greyhound Bus station. Hunted for a room for Honey. Wound up at Mrs. Williams—$2 per nite.

Wednesday 12th: Birthday—spent a memorable day with Honey.

Thursday: Another long day to be remembered.

Friday: Went to Bay City with Honey. Came home 4:30 pm. Practiced and missed Honey so much—went to bed with his name on my lips.

Saturday: Lonesome. Stayed in bed until 4 pm—wrote letters—ate—went to show at Franklin—saw "Lost Angel." Called Mrs. Williams. Spent evening at her home. Toured "ward" (colored neighborhood). Home at 11 pm. End of a lonesome day.

Sunday: 11:30 am Zion Baptist Church, Saginaw. 3:30 Musical Rev. E.B. Johnson. Had a pleasant day with Roberta. Missed Honey so, so much. Daydreamed all day. Thanks to Roberta and Luther, I snapped out of it. Got in at 10 pm and washed.

Monday: Hairdresser appt at 9 cancelled.

Tuesday: Got up late. Hairdresser appt at 10 am changed to 4:30 pm. Another letter from Honey. Invited to a card party.

Wednesday: Went to show. Nothing exciting. Loving and missing Honey so much.

Thursday: Letter from Honey. 1 pm—lunched with Mrs. Hood. 6 pm—met a YM resident at Cunningham. 6:45 pm—called for in fine car—taken to party given for me at Mrs. Eva Wilson's home. Refreshments and liquor served— received gift, a blue box of stationery.

Friday: Supper 60 cents for 2 hamburgers with Betty in room—and Pepsi Cola. Both of us wound up sick with gas. Mrs. Williams sick—went to see if I could be of any assistance.

Saturday: Got up 10 am. Lunch 11. Shopped for Mrs. Williams. Came home and waited for Betty. Dinner at 6:30 at Canton. Went to show and washed.

Sunday: Dinner at Mrs. Williams—Luther's birthday. Drive to Bay City. Drank one glass beer—2 small wines—2 eggnogs—sick at nite. Bets came in at 1:30 am—talked until 3 am. Bat came in through bathroom window. Stayed up to 4:30 shooing bat out.

Monday: Washed and ironed—breakfasted. Had dinner with Bets at Canton— party at Williams.

Tuesday: Up at 5 am to catch 6:45 am train to Traverse City. Just made it by a split second. Bill Williams and Martha very, very kind to me. Arrived Traverse City. Took bus to Kervadin. Walked right up on Honey in orchard. Helped pick a few cherries. Got bags and bunked with Wilma (Mrs. Clinton DeForest) in trailer.

Wednesday: Up at 5 am. Slept in trailer—had a good nite's rest—just knowing I was that close to Honey. Met him at orchard at 6 am. Worked and had lunch together. He went his way and I mine. Talked and kissed on grass until 10 pm. Love bug bitten me badly.

Thursday: Rained and worked picking cherries in orchard with Honey— didn't mind rain one bit knowing Honey was by my side.

Friday: Still raining and very windy. Went to orchard around noon. Took Honey lunch.

Saturday: Picked cherries from 9 am—1 pm. Tired—basked in sun all pm. Had a nice dinner ready.

Sunday: Rested all am. Honey came to see me. Invited Michael Isaacs to dinner. Burnt rice—managed anyway. Dinner turned out swell—Honey said it was nice.

Monday: Up at 8:30 am. Went to orchard at 10 am. Fixed lunch and dinner. Usual evening. Mrs. Pat Raeburn baked cherry pie—35 cents.

Tuesday, August 1ˢᵗ: Holiday—boys sad because they had to work. Lunch and dinner same. Still loving Honey more and more.

Wednesday: Usual routine at orchard. Mrs. Williams gave John and I a cherry pie—was very good with dinner. Had ice cream.

Thursday: Honey worked at another orchard 35 miles from here. I stayed home—missed Honey so much. "If he only knew" etc. Had dinner together with Wilma and Kitty. Worried about him because he had no lunch or money. Poor thing.

Friday: Still at F Orchard. Spent an anxious day waiting and waiting. Cried and wondered what could have happened to my Honey. At 9:15 the phone rang. Honey explained he had to settle some dispute. I loved him so much I forgave him for keeping me worried.

Saturday: Honey worked on KP duty outside my door. Since I got no kiss this a.m. I am dying for one—anxiously waiting for Honey so I can collect. May go to town later. Had dinner. Decided to stay home and hold hands. Spent evening loving up til midnight.

Sunday August 6: Sunbathed and read 2 stories today. Loving him oh so much—so much until it hurts. Have never met so nice a person. Every hour he tells me he loves me—all so heavenly. Visited the Rayburns—discussed everything from soup to nuts. Honey well versed in politics. I am so proud of him.

Monday August 7: Sent G.B.T. special delivery birthday message from John and I. Honey woke me—he went shopping for us. No work today—hallelujah!

Tuesday August 8: Fine living all day. No work for Honey.

Wednesday 9th: Boys still awaiting transfer. Loving from morning til nite— especially nite. Cooked dinner. Still loving him more and more.

Thursday 10th: Honey and I went shopping.

Friday 11th: Got up early to get Honey's breakfast so he wouldn't get gas— since I had been bad giving him breakfast late. Telegram from Mom. Honey still a nice boy.

Saturday 12th: Honey went to work after breakfast. Had dinner ready for once on time. Went shopping with boys in Elk Rapids and to show "Jam Session and 2-man Submarine." Enjoyed a delightful evening with Honey by my side.

Sunday 13th: Stayed in bed until almost noon. Brunched at 1 with Honey. Loved under maple trees until quite late—dinner at 7 pm. No company (thank heavens)—a day alone.

Monday 14th: On K.P. Honey relaxed while I washed. Had 6 boys from company under maple tree. Read to 2 boys and Honey. Cooke and Walter usual evening guests. Scanned Spiegel's order catalog—went to bed quietly— tired.

Tuesday 15: Cooke, Walter, Honey and I went to Traverse City. Honey placed engagement ring on finger. Girl I was so happy. Usual loving accompanied evening. Had dinner—then a heavy wind storm cutting off electricity and water. Went to bed by oil lamp. Such fun.

Wednesday 16th: Woke up at 6 am—went back to bed. Dreamt Momma raised hell because I had spent all day loving and made Sondra run away. Whew—it was good to wake up in Honey's arms. If this is heaven, let me die now.

Mom and Dad, out on a date

Thursday 17: Honey made me sleep late. Had breakfast all ready when I awoke. It was so sweet of Honey and a delicious breakfast too. Had Cooke, Walter, Wimpy and Samuel to lunch. Harold and Pat had wine with me later.

Friday 18th: Honey woke up with toothache. Made him stay in bed. Doctored his tooth and he felt better. Left suddenly at 3 pm for Traverse City. Traveled on same train for Grand Rapids from 5 pm to 11:30 pm. A happy parting on train—Honey was quite sleepy. Had he been wide awake he might have insisted that I spend the nite with him at Grand Rapids. But fearing possible connection, grabbed awaiting train bound for Detroit. Arrived Detroit 6:10 am. Saw Walker, Isaac and Wimpy Samuels and learned that Honey had to remain in Grand Rapids until noon today. Shucks—had I known, I could have stayed in Grand Rapids and caught a later train. Now the problem is—how can I make a connection—nearly at wit's end, when found that all seats enroute NY had been reserved. Fortunately, there was an unreserved coach to Buffalo. At least I will see Buffalo in daylight—passed through Canada (Windsor, St. Thomas). Beautiful journey—and missing Honey so much. 12:30 pm passing Niagara Falls. 1:00 pm left Canada. 1:15 pm Buffalo—lunched with friends I met on the train—took 2:15 pm train (Dewitt Clinton) enroute direct NY. Arrived NY 11:59 pm. Home at 1:00 am. The end of a perfect vacation.

The Journal: 1944

After becoming engaged in Saginaw, we parted. I returned to Brooklyn. John followed for wedding ceremony October 7, 1944. Rev. George Stark from Siloam officiated. The ceremony was held at 298 Greene in the parlor room. The reception was held downstairs in the dining room. My sister Gloria was the matron of honor. My best friend, Muriel Williams, was the maid of honor. And of course, Dorrell Buddle was the best man. We spent our honeymoon at Ada Martin's home at 111 West 118th Street in Harlem.

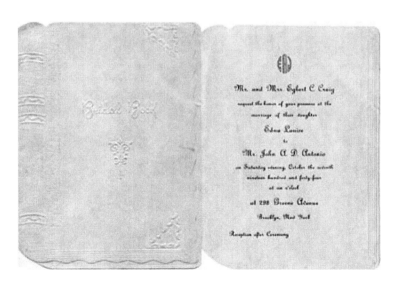

The wedding invitation

The wedding. Top row: Dad's brother, Vivian; Dad; Dad's best friend, Dorrell Buddle Middle row: Mom's sister, Gloria; Mom; Mom's best friend, Muriel Williams Front row: Gloria's daughter, Sondra, the flower girl

The Journal: Looking back on the years 1940-1952

During the past ten years, my Dad—according to his version—was not being adequately spiritually fed. He decided to transfer his membership to a Pentecostal church at 284 Greene Avenue. As a dedicated wife, my mom did likewise. Gloria stayed at St. Peter Clavers until she drifted out of the church altogether. During these years, I became a free-lance musician (pianist) to Refuge Pentecostal Church, Holy Trinity Church, BYPU (Baptist Young People's Union) and several other Pentecostal churches. I also found time on Friday evenings to act as pianist for the Battalion of Prayer, a small prayer group on Greene Avenue near Marcy.

Dr. Charles Francis McCoy was a pastor, as well as a good friend of my father's. On several occasions I was guest organist at Dr. McCoy's church in Oyster Bay, New York. When Dr. McCoy started his radio ministry, I was the accompanying pianist. I did have a keen eye for sight-reading which proved helpful, especially when soloists failed to show up for rehearsals. I held these positions through the 1940s. In retrospect, how I ever carried such a workload is almost unbelievable.

In addition, I became a board member of the Brooklyn Home for the Aged (St. John's Place), becoming very active under the chair of Mrs. Anne Yearwood for more years than I care to remember. I was then in my early 20's and enjoying each position.

At Siloam, I chaired a committee to raise funds for a new pipe organ, a 2-year $40,000 campaign, which was successful. Florence Mills, then the organist, took ill and I was once again called upon to be the Acting Organist. It was fascinating greeting competitors of this position. I vividly recall one applicant, playing his own composition of a well-known hymn, using only foot pedals. Absolutely fascinating! Carleton Inniss, a young schoolteacher and musician, was hired. I bowed out after he settled in.

By this time, the choir had reached professional standards and Dorothy Sullivan replaced me as assistant organist. As far as I know, she still holds this position. It may be interesting to here note that I received $35 for each service.

In 1952, I was ordained an elder by the Presbytery of Siloam Church. I continued assisting Mr. Inniss with the choir practices.

In 1983, I left Siloam to escort my aging mother to her birthplace in Montego Bay, where we remained until 1996. I terminated my membership at Siloam, primarily because Presbyterians required the church to pay a tax for each attending member. I felt obliged to remove my name from the membership rolls. Sad to say, at present, I am not a member of any church, but nonetheless, I maintain strong ties with several members at age 79.

Cheryl: My Memories of Siloam

My father and I attended a church in Queens, while Toots continued to attend Siloam Presbyterian Church. They often had special concerts and choir practice on Saturdays. Often, when I was about 6 or 7, I accompanied my mother to these practices. Carleton Inniss was the choir director and my mother played the organ. This was one of those original pipe organs, with tall copper pipes lining both walls of the choir loft. It was the loudest, yet most melodious instrument I have ever heard. It made a big, booming noise, discordant and harmonious at the same time.

Mr. Inniss had three daughters: Debbie, Julia and Carla. Often, they also came to the church on Saturdays. I remember running around the church, laughing and playing hide-and-seek with them, sometimes jumping when the organ was particularly loud. I was between Julia and Carla in age; Debbie was older—I don't ever remember her getting into mischief like we did. Every so often, Mr. Inniss would turn around and bellow "Girls—behave yourselves!" which usually kept us quiet for about five minutes, at the most. Carleton and Gloria Inniss and their family remained close friends of our family for years. I had the pleasure of taking my dad to Gloria's surprise 80th birthday party, although by that time he didn't understand who she was or why we were even there.

The Journal: 1964

Second show of generosity by my mother to me. I worked at the YWCA on an 11-month contract. I had one month's vacation from the office plus I took an extra month every summer. This arrangement made it possible for Cheryl, our second daughter, and I to take our usual summer vacation to Jamaica to visit my parents. This particular summer, when Cheryl was 8 years of age, my mother suggested we visit Panama. She gave me $1000 to travel to see her sister, Aunt Lou. What a splendid experience. We had reservations to stay at a very old army mansion with high gates and ceiling-to-floor windows. We spent one night here. After Mrs. Nell Rankin heard we were visiting, she insisted we spend the entire visit at her home (typically Spanish). The adults in the home were very impressed with Cheryl's 8-year-old mentality—able to converse with each adult.

All in all, it was a very pleasant change from the mundane visits and people of Jamaica. The Panamanians were far more intelligent and far more gracious. As a result of this visit, Aunt Lou (Louise) visited Montego Bay to see her sister (my mom).

I remember this trip like it was yesterday. We first flew from Montego Bay to Barranquilla, Columbia to change planes enroute to Panama. I remember we had an extremely long layover at the airport and we were quite bored. When we finally arrived in Panama, the hotel was a remodeled fort hundreds of years old. Huge rusty cannons lined a huge lawn overlooking the ocean. The front desk gave us a large, heavy, rusty room key. We were left on our own to roam the cavernous hallways and find our own room, which was spacious but stuffy. The windows were floor-to-ceiling and when we opened one, we were greeted with a blast of the sea breeze that blew the curtains way up to the ceiling. The hotel was really in the middle of nowhere so we were stuck there for the evening. We had dinner in a very elegant dining room. I remember my mother being disappointed at not being able to get a decent cup of coffee. Fortunately, we only spent one night there and took the train the next day to Colon, where we met up with the Rankin family. There always seemed to be a lot of children around and I played with them. Despite the language barrier—I spoke only English and French, and the children only Spanish—we soon discovered that we knew the same games. I had a great time and was very impressed that our visit actually made the local papers. I was enormously proud seeing our names in print.

New Yorker Ends Vacation Abroad

COLON — Mrs. Edna C. Antonio, accompanied by her eight-year-old daughter, Cheryl, was scheduled to leave Jamaica yesterday for New York after a week's holiday.

The Antonios previously spent a week in Panama before leaving for the Caribbean Isle of Springs, where they were the guests of Mrs. Antonio's mother, Mrs. Ivy Craig, a resident of Montego Bay, St. James.

While here the visitors were the guests of the Rankine family, on 7th Street and Melendez avenue.

Newspaper clipping from local paper, Colon, Panama

Travels with Toots

Working in the travel industry has its benefits. I was fortunate to have been able to take my parents on quite a few vacations. When I worked for KLM, occasionally one of them would accompany me on a business trip to Amsterdam.

I lived in Amsterdam for a year, from August 1994 to August 1995. At the time, my parents had already retired and were living in Montego Bay. In the spring, I invited them to Amsterdam for a 3-week visit. I had rented a beautiful furnished apartment overlooking a canal in the front and a garden in the back. The only difficulty was the steep and winding staircase, so typical of Dutch buildings.

We took an overnight train to Nice and boarded a ship for a weeklong Mediterranean cruise. We shared a cabin—I had the top bunk. We had a great time. The banter between my parents provided hours of entertainment for me. Even at that time, however, Mom's legs started bothering her and she preferred to plant herself in a sunny spot. She was content to sit and write letters and postcards while Dad and I took advantage of exploring every port. We always brought back a souvenir for her—a lace handkerchief or a fan. ("A lady never sweats—only perspires—and must always have a fan handy.")

When we got back to the ship, we would find Mom usually in the same spot we had left her. But she would be surrounded by an entourage of "new friends." She was like a queen on her throne, holding court. She attracted people like a magnet—always cordial and polite to everyone except "drinkers"—she found them to be loud and obnoxious. People who couldn't hold their liquor lacked self-discipline, a sign of some underlying character defect. Other than that, she was tolerant of anyone's race, religion, political belief or background. She didn't care where you came from or what you did. As long as you conducted yourself properly, like a lady or a gentleman, you were forever included in her circle of friends.

We took many other trips together, including Rome and the Amalfi Coast and Williamsburg Virginia. Just the two of us went to Amsterdam, Connecticut and New Orleans. We both liked to do the same things—eat, sleep and shop—so there was never any lack of activity. We could sit and talk for hours and do nothing else.

After my parents retired to Jamaica, they took several Caribbean and South American cruises. It seems like everyone they met and befriended on cruises ended up on Mom's writing list. When I went through her address book, calling her friends to advise them of her passing, so many of them said, "We met your parents years ago on a cruise and your mother has been writing us ever since."

Photos I took of Toots and Dad on our travels together

...on the Via Veneto, Rome, 1986

...in front of a castle in Zeist, the Netherlands, 1995

... on Mediterranean cruise, spring 1995

Jean

My sister started showing symptoms of illness at age 2. My mother said she knew something was wrong, but the doctors were stumped. By the time she was 4, Jean was diagnosed with leukemia and spent time in and out of the hospitals. The doctors wanted to try all sorts of experimental treatments on Jean; they told my parents they were on the verge of discovering the cure for leukemia. This was in 1955. It's now more than 50 years later, and they are no closer to a cure. Nevertheless, her health continued to decline and she died when she was 5.

My sister Jean's illness and death affected many people, among them my mother's friend, Myrtle Levy James. She remembers the Saturday that my mother called to say that Jean had been diagnosed with leukemia. The next day, Myrtle took the train to Brooklyn Hospital to sit with Jean and Mom. Of Jean: "She was a precious little girl. I'll never forget that white casket. It took so much out of me because my Reggie was the same age." Myrtle had been a nurse at Montefiore Hospital; after my sister's death, she stopped taking care of children in the hospital.

At the time, my mother told everyone that it was a good thing that Jean had died; she didn't want her daughter to suffer and she didn't believe the doctors were helping her. Everyone must have thought my mother had lost her mind; she must have been overcome with grief to say such a thing. Even my father disagreed with her. Looking back, she had the right attitude and she overcame my sister's death quickly, whereas my father never stopped grieving for his first child.

When Jean died, I was 10 months old. There's only one picture that I know of the two of us. It was a formal portrait taken at Abraham & Strauss, a downtown Brooklyn department store. As the story goes, the photographer wouldn't take the picture because I was only 2 months old at the time and he didn't trust Jean to hold me. But my mother said that she was dying so the photographer finally agreed to take the picture. For years, I walked around with that picture in my wallet, wondering why I was alive and she wasn't.

Me and Jean

My father was an amateur photographer himself and took hundreds of pictures of Jean at their favorite spot, the Brooklyn Botanical Gardens. After she died, he put his cameras and equipment away in the basement and never took another picture.

My mother and Jean, Brooklyn Botanical Gardens, 1955

Cheryl

I found it interesting that there was very little mention of my childhood in my mother's journal, except for the trip to Panama. I guess I am almost more intrigued by what she did not say rather than what she did write down. What would she have said of me? Would she have thought I was a good daughter? Did she think I was just like her? Telephone callers often could not tell us apart. My friends say I write like her. Even now, when I speak, often is it my mother's words and inflections that leap from my lips. And when I look in the bathroom mirror, I am sometimes shocked to see my mother's reflection staring back at me.

Mom and me, June 1957. I am 9 months old

I knew she thought I was a well-mannered child. She made sure of that. My mother was the queen of etiquette. We read books together on table settings, manners in general, how gentlemen should treat ladies. At seven, I knew the difference between a salad fork and a shellfish fork and could set a formal dining table. Mom taught me that when shaking hands, it is always up to the lady to offer her hand first to a gentleman. A man should never extend his hand first; that would be a rude assumption on his part that the lady would indeed want to touch him.

There were no such things as temper tantrums or speaking back to adults. Manners were very important to her, a sign of "good breeding." Ladies never went out without their hat and gloves. If you didn't have anything intelligent to offer during a conversation, then you were supposed to keep quiet and listen—perhaps you would learn a thing or two. However, a real lady would be intelligent and know a little about every subject in order to be able to contribute to any conversation. A knowledge of the arts was particularly useful for this.

Mastery of music and at least one foreign language were essential. My early childhood storybooks, including *Goldilocks and the Three Bears* and *Little Red Riding Hood*, were all in French. Saturday mornings were reserved for piano lessons. Saturday afternoons were for cultural expeditions.

I can recall hundreds of wonderful afternoons spent at the Brooklyn Academy of Music. Sometimes, we would go to Lincoln Center and pay $2.00 for standing room at performances. Once the lights dimmed, you were allowed to take any available seats in the balcony. My favorite performance was the Russian ballet—I was mesmerized. One number was performed with the dancers wearing big black cloaks and gliding as if they were moving on air. I despised opera, so that was quickly ruled out as an option. On other occasions, we went to museums, our favorites being the Brooklyn Museum and the Museum of Natural History.

If we couldn't find any interesting performances to attend, there was always shopping. Best & Co., Lord & Taylor and B. Altman's were our favorite stores. Mom had credit cards at all three. She firmly believed in paying more for quality products that would last—"You can always tell good things," she used to say. When I was a teenager, she would write a letter to the department stores authorizing me to use her credit card. No spending limits were ever imposed and she trusted my judgment implicitly. No matter what I brought home, she never made a comment. At the stores, armed with credit card and letter in hand, I always felt like a millionaire.

The most important childhood lesson I learned was to treat everyone with respect, because "but for the grace of God, there you go." I grew up in the Fort Greene/Clinton Hill section of Brooklyn, a racially mixed, middle-class neighborhood. There wasn't much crime in the neighborhood; we were never afraid of walking the streets at night, but we seemed to have a lot of drunks lying around on the sidewalks. I will never forget my mother's words: "Step over them if you must but always say 'Good Morning.'" I can't ever recall not even one who, despite his inebriated state, didn't tip his hat or reply "Good Morning ma'am" back. I learned if you treat people with respect, you earn their respect in return.

Toots never cared what other people thought of her and taught me to do the same. What you thought of yourself was much more important. Sometimes she did things that I thought were odd. Looking back, I see that she was just expressing herself in her own unique way.

Everyone always admits to being embarrassed of their parents at some point in their youth. We always think our parents are old-fashioned and that they don't know anything. How could they? Having grown up with black-and-white television, no Internet, no computers, no iPods. Gee—they mostly read books, didn't they? Every generation considers itself more sophisticated than the last. Yet, now I realize that wisdom—knowledge through experience—is something that can't be learned through any technological gadget, and looking back, we now all acknowledge how wise our parents really were.

My mother had some eccentric moments during my school years. I know for sure my mother didn't think she was the world's greatest mother. Even as a child, I recognized that she was weak in a lot of areas you depend on your mother to be. Along the way, mothers play many roles in our lives: cooks, nurses, hairdressers, chaperones, disciplinarians, fashion coordinators, the "birds-and-the-bees" advisors, counselors and advocates. Sometimes, I found her parenting skills lacking in many of those areas.

Cook? Our dinner menus were very limited. She blamed my father's ulcers for the fact that she had to cook bland food. Looking back, I realize how she probably just didn't like cooking so she cooked the same things over and over.

Nurse? The sight of blood made her squeamish. At five, I learned how to bandage my own cuts because she wouldn't do it for me.

Hairdresser? Until I went to high school, I wore my hair the same way every day—two long braids which were always lopsided and the part in my hair was always uneven. I used to look forward to my cousin Sondra coming over. She would brush my braids out and redo them evenly. My hair would look so nice my mother wouldn't put a brush to my head for a week for fear that she would have to re-braid it. Finally, when my head started to look like a bird's nest, Mom would break down and attempt to comb it again. One day when I was twelve, I couldn't stand the look of despair on her face anymore, and I announced that from then on I would do my own hair. "Oh, good" was her only comment. She handed me the brush and that was the last time she ever touched my hair.

Chaperone? She trusted me implicitly and never asked me where I was or who I was with, even as an adult. Toots preferred to put money in my hand and tell me to go and have a good time. She truly believed not knowing was the best defense.

Disciplinarian? By age seven, I realized Dad was the one I had to worry about; he was a firm believer in "Spare the rod and spoil the child." Toots was too busy to worry about correcting any minor infraction I might have incurred. During high school, I had the feeling she was trying to be more a sister to me than a mother. Spurred on by high school friends who were experimenting with all sorts of things (cigarettes, drugs, boyfriends, girlfriends), I desperately wanted a mother who would tell me, in no uncertain terms, what to do and what not to do. Toots was not that mother. No matter what I confessed to doing, her constant reply: "Don't let your father find out." She was the best secret-keeper, though. No matter what I told her, she never once ratted me out to Dad. Of course, her implied approval only inspired me to be even more reckless. By the time I was twenty, I was convinced I was, like her, invincible.

Fashion coordinator? When she picked out my clothes for grade school, they were never color-coordinated. I clearly remember one day in the fourth grade: I had on an orange sweater and a purple skirt with black socks. I remember looking down at myself and thinking well at least the colors were pretty even if I didn't match so well. One of the happiest days of my childhood was the day I started Catholic high school and had to wear a uniform every day. It relieved us both of the agony of having to dress me.

Explaining the birds and the bees? Toots handed my friend, Denise, and me a book about sex—I think we were about 10. I remember the book—it talked about farm animals; I don't think it ever mentioned humans, but we quickly understood what the point was. All we did was giggle. The book was never mentioned again. When I was 13, Toots attempted to explain the facts of life. This normally conversant woman was stumbling and stuttering so badly that I finally said, "It's okay Mom. You don't have to tell me. I already know." She asked, "Where did you learn this?" "In the streets, like everyone else," I replied. Well—that was the end of that discussion.

Counselor? Advocate? In those respects, I couldn't have asked for a better mother. I always got the feeling that she didn't like to be asked for advice. Sometimes, I would ask a question and she would deliberately change the subject, just so she wouldn't have to answer me. Instead, she encouraged me to think on my own and trust my instinct. Experience would be my best teacher, so she wasn't afraid to let me make a mistake. And boy, did I make lots of mistakes. But she never criticized my decisions; she always let me find my own path, and so I grew up thinking I would never know if something would work or not unless I tried it. It might work, it might not, but I would survive either way. In martial arts, one of the tenets is Indomitable Spirit. Webster's defines indomitable as "incapable of being subdued; unconquerable." If I could define my mother with one word, it would be that word: indomitable. If I inherited nothing else from her, that indomitable spirit was the greatest gift. In Sunday school we memorized "I can do all things through Christ who strengthens me," but it was my mother who showed me just how that unconquerable spirit works by her example.

Mom and me, taken in front of our house on Tate Street, Montego Bay, Jamaica, 1984

During my master's program, I had the privilege of taking two courses with the best professor I ever had, Dr. Donald Wetmore. One day in class, he told us to write on one side of a card—"Don't sweat the small stuff." And on the other side of the card—"It's ALL small stuff." And then it hit me—that's what Toots had been talking about her whole life. Expending energy was for helping others, not worrying about what happened yesterday or what might happen tomorrow. She truly believed Matthew 6.34: So don't be anxious about tomorrow. God will take care of your tomorrow too. Live one day at a time (The Living Bible).

Although she didn't have a great sense of humor, she often made me laugh just by her actions. Toots finally got the nerve up to take driving lessons when she was in her forties. One day, she picked me up from P.S. 11 in our family's Rambler. Her driving was slow but she wasn't reckless—she didn't care how many cars were honking behind her. But her parking skills were abominable, a deficiency I seem to have inherited. Something about calculating the angles—see, there's that math problem again. Anyway, it must have taken her half an hour to park the car. And she wouldn't let me get out of the car until it was parked perfectly. Sheepishly, I thanked her for picking me up at school but told her that I would prefer to walk home from then on. I can't recall her driving anywhere after that.

We always had a dog or two in the family, among other assorted pets, including fish, hamsters, and rabbits. One day, Mom picked me up after school with our pet rabbit on a leash. All the other kids in school thought the rabbit was cute, but I thought it was the dumbest thing I had ever seen. I begged her to please leave the rabbit at home.

My junior high school years were spent at JHS 117. The neighborhood was fine, but the students were hoodlums. I walked about a half-mile to school in fear every single day. Being two years younger than everyone else in my grade and being short made me an easy target for bullies. One day in the playground, I left my schoolbooks on a bench. To my horror, some students lit firecrackers on top of my books and I watched them burn. I was petrified to go to school after that, although I put on a brave front. When my mother started showing up after school to escort me home, I don't know if I was more comforted by her presence or mortified by the fact that everyone knew my mother was picking me up. She never explained why she was there or how she knew I was scared. But she was a big woman and I knew nobody would mess with me anymore.

Mom also wasn't big on neatness. Not once did she ever ask me to clean my room. In Jamaica, we had maids and I wasn't even allowed to make my bed, as I have mentioned—a habit I carried all throughout the year. On the rare occasion when company was coming, my idea of cleaning was to throw everything under the bed and on the closet floor. She would look at the pile of clothes on the floor and never say a word. My husband will attest to the fact that I have made very little progress in that area.

Mom was Queen of the Shopping Catalogs. She would order anything and everything, mostly novelties and trinkets. Every time she would ask Dad for the checkbook, he would ask, "What junk are you buying now?" She always replied "Never mind—you don't need to know." Most of the time, it really was junk and broke after the first use or she never even used it at all. If it were defective or cheap, she would write the company immediately. Usually, she got her money back or free coupons for more junk.

Occasionally, something actually useful would make it into our house. One such item was a long plastic pole with a hinged grabbing mechanism on the end. She used it to pick stuff up off the floor without having to bend over. One day, something fell behind the refrigerator and didn't we have to use that contraption. It came in handy after all. Even Dad chuckled.

One year, she put a potato masher in my husband Gary's Christmas stocking. To my knowledge, Gary has never mashed a potato in his life. Every time I use it, we chuckle, "What was she thinking??"

As I reviewed pictures and memories in putting this memoir together, I realize there was one constant factor throughout our home—humor. My parents never raised their voices at each other. Rather, they pandered with each other—sarcasm with a smile, if you will.

She taught me to always look on the bright side of life and to pluck out the best part of any situation. Deal with the distasteful circumstances that come your way, laugh about the rest, and then move on. We laughed together, the three of us, until our sides hurt, especially on trips.

Of the two, my mother definitely had the more positive attitude. "Hold your head up high" she constantly chided me. She believed in taking risks—everything was supposed to be an adventure. Dad was a man of strict routine. Toots was haphazard—sleep whenever, eat whatever, up at 1 am writing notes, up at 4 a.m. watching TV. Dad was a quiet man. Toots never stopped talking. It didn't matter if you were watching TV, eating dinner, trying to sleep—she kept up an endless stream of chatter, not necessarily waiting for a reply.

I swear my mother was telepathic. Whenever I telephoned, no matter what time of day or night, she always answered the phone "Hello darling." Even though I knew the answer I would still always ask, "How did you know it was me?" "I always know when it's you" she would reply. That always baffled me. I still feel like she is watching me.

Music, Continued

One of her greatest accomplishments was becoming President of the Brooklyn Symphony Orchestra in the early '70s. The conductor and my mother worked well together. He and his wife often came to our house for dinner. Toots was responsible for organizing the concerts, soliciting donors, all correspondence, coordinating refreshments during the concert break, and other duties. She had a huge desk brought into her bedroom and she worked tirelessly for hours to promote the Orchestra. Occasionally, I helped her with the typing and labeling. The concerts were held Sunday afternoons at St. Peter Clavers in Brooklyn, and although I really didn't appreciate classical musical performances, I always enjoyed attending the concerts, just to see everyone turned out in their Sunday best.

During the late '70s, Mom started sporadically attending the same church as Dad and me. She never played either the piano or the organ there. However, that all changed one Easter Sunday morning. Between the two morning services, breakfast was served downstairs in the fellowship hall. After breakfast, people would drift slowly back up to the sanctuary, waiting for the 10:45 am service to start. Mom became annoyed at all the noise people were making in the sanctuary, chatting and moving around. So she took out a hymnbook, sat down at the piano, and began to play. In a few minutes, her playing had the desired effect and people took their seats quietly. Very few people at the church had ever even heard my mother play before.

Her "musical interlude" became a yearly tradition at the pastor's request. One of my favorite memories was helping her pick out songs for the concert. For weeks before Easter, we would go through her repertoire and pick out hymns as well as classical arrangements. During the concert, I performed my usual role of page-turner. Sitting next to her on the piano bench made me feel as if, in some small way, the concert was my contribution as well as hers. I was immensely proud of her musical ability and felt privileged just to share in the spotlight.

After many years of performing, she suggested to the pastor that younger people should take over the musical interlude. And for several years, other talented members of the congregation played instruments and sang during that time.

*Toots playing the Wissner Baby Grand at my
parents' 55th wedding anniversary party.
Queens, New York, October 1999*

The Jamaica Years: 1983-1996

In 1982, my dad retired from the job he had held for more than 40 years. My parents decided to retire to Montego Bay to enjoy the warmer weather and the slower pace of life. My mother had lived at 298 Greene for 57 years and it was not an easy decision for her to sell the house. Nevertheless, she acquiesced and they began to make plans to move.

In April 1983, the freight forwarders came and took all their furniture and belongings to be shipped first to Kingston, where they would clear customs, and then by truck to Montego Bay. In May, I surprised my parents with first-class tickets on American Airlines and we all flew down to MoBay. I had just started my job at KLM the month before so I only had a 4-day weekend off. It was a tearful parting at the MoBay airport that last day; we had never been apart before. I think I cried the entire flight home. I was 26, divorced, with a new job, new home, no brothers or sisters, and for the first time in my life, I felt completely on my own. Almost every four-day weekend, I would fly down to visit my parents. As an airline employee, I could travel stand-by on Eastern Airlines for $50 round-trip. If I was in the mood to splurge, I bought a ticket on American Airlines for $100. They alternated holiday visits to New York. We seldom went two months without seeing each other. We also signaled each other every day. Whenever I came home, I would dial them and let the phone ring once, then hang up. They would dial back and hang up after one ring. It was our way of saying hello every single day.

Life in Montego Bay turned out to be not quite what they expected. As the saying goes, it's a nice place to visit, but...

Dad had to go downtown and stand on long lines to pay electric and telephone bills. The lines weren't always organized and orderly and there was a lot of pushing and shoving. No place for an elderly man.

The electric service was constantly interrupted. The authorities would black out the residential areas to make sure there was enough power for the tourist resorts (these were the days before resorts had their own generators). Plenty of candles and kerosene lamps had to be kept on hand. No more than two days' worth of food could be kept in the refrigerator, so there wouldn't be too much to throw out in case the power was off for more than a day.

Sometimes the water service was cut off for a day. No bathing, no washing dishes, no ice. Just a bucket of saved water for emergency use.

Some of the housekeepers they hired proved to be less than trustworthy. One stole *all* of Dad's long-sleeved white shirts after her first (and last) week working there.

Almost all of the food in Jamaica is imported from somewhere else, much of it from the U.S. Their favorite foods and brands were hard to come by, and when available, at an exorbitant cost. I kept lots of clothes in Jamaica so my carry-on bag was always packed with goodies for them—Postum and Entenmann's for Dad, Maxwell House coffee and Wheat Thins for Toots. I always tried to smuggle in restricted foods that my parents loved and couldn't get in Jamaica. Most of the times I made it past customs without any problems, and only twice in the 13 years they lived there were the foods confiscated at the airport. Once Dad complained that he missed lamb chops and on my next trip, I tried getting through with a package of frozen chops wrapped in several layers of Saran Wrap and strapped tightly around my waist under a very loose blouse. It worked quite nicely and over the years, I took steaks, turkey for Thanksgiving, lamb and pork chops, and once I got through with a whole ham.

The heat didn't seem to bother Dad too much, but it sapped Toots' energy. By 1991, her electrolytes were so low she almost went into a coma. The doctor in Montego Bay didn't even know what was wrong with her (diagnosed as Guillain Barre syndrome here) and urged me to take her to New York for treatment. She had to be air ambulanced and spent a year here recuperating. The medical facilities in Jamaica were appalling (one of my cousins died in the emergency waiting room at the hospital; she had been waiting for more than 24 hours to be seen).

Dad once told me he had gone to the dentist who apologized, saying that he was out of Novocain and hadn't had any for over a year. I was horrified and insisted that they come to New York for all their check-ups and dental visits.

Most of all, what bothered Toots were the people's attitudes. She found most Jamaicans to be rude and ungrateful, always looking for a handout. She never did adjust to people being consistently late, not saying "thank-you" and never reciprocating small acts of kindness. I think she missed her friends here and never really adjusted to "island life."

Eventually, in 1996, I convinced them to return to New York. Their increased need for good medical care and the obvious lack of facilities in Jamaica made the decision easy. Besides, crime was on the increase in

Montego Bay and I was concerned over their safety. We couldn't "assume the position" on the front porch after dark anymore; there were too many shady characters coming up to the front gate looking for a handout or claiming to be a long-lost relative or friend. I wasn't happy that Dad would go out to church at night and leave Toots alone at home (the maids only worked during the day).

My dad, "assuming the position," on the front porch of our house in Montego Bay

While my parents were in Jamaica, my mother wrote me every day. Not a day passed when there wasn't a letter in my mailbox to greet me when I came home from work. And if there were a delay in the mail, the next day I would receive two. Sometimes she insisted that Dad add a note at the end of the letter.

What follows are excerpts from some of the letters I kept.

Thurs Oct 1, '87

Dearest Missy,

Just exchanged our zings. A full day yesterday—going to Bogue [a suburb of Montego Bay] *then to the lawyers to sign some papers.*

Beryl [Dad's youngest sister- she had Alzheimer's] *was asleep but Dad and I looked in on her—she does look frail—very frail—only skin and bones. Inez* [Dad's oldest sister] *the same. Not much new to report today. Uncle Jr. was here yesterday. I gave him the Daily News. I commented on how good he looked. No comment.*

Wow! Dad and I ate all our chicken (except one leg)—Willem's recipe. Terrific—I shall write George [friends from Port Washington] *as soon as I get myself together. I want you to know Baskin-Robbins and your apple pie are reducing.*

Yesterday, Zaidie said that I lost weight and when I went to visit the Browns (8 Tate), they knew I lost weight. Hip hip hooray. I've been following your advice—no bread.

Dad sez Ruth [one of the housekeepers] *is not so bad. I thought he wanted her to go. At least she is trustworthy and knows her place. She was so thrilled over the things you sent for her.*

Oh dear October is already here. Do you plan to travel here??

All for now love

Affectionately, Dad and Toots

Friday April 29, '88

Hi baby,

Here we are sweating at 8 am. I could do well with some cool mornings here. All's well so far. Going to Bogue today and will go to the beach tomorrow.

It was so wonderful to spend the 4 weeks with you. I enjoyed every day of it. Do hope we will be able to do this for a long time yet. Do hope Misty [my car] *is doing alright.*

Love

Dad

Dad and me

Thurs 9/28/88, "the day after"

Darling Missy,

How very wonderful to have had you for four delightful days. As I said to Dad, we crowded four weeks of activities and conversation into four beautiful days.

I spent too much time—thinking of each day's meals and Dad that we completely forgot to give you your birthday gift. What a sad commentary. When I reminded Dad last nite, he nearly fell through the floor. And I neglected to place a little love note in your hand luggage. Could that be signs of growing up too rapidly? I was so intent on playing the piano for you, I completely forgot my usual love note.

7 a.m.: I am walking to the downtown P.O. to find out if there is any kind of speed mail service from here. I somehow remember Helga using a speed-mail service from NY (containing Carol's immigration papers) and the letter was delivered right to the door. I'll check into this.

It was a real real delight having you darling.

Each time the phone rang—circa 6, 7 & 8 p.m.—I said, "It's Cher—calling collect from Miami."

And thank you again for all the delicious treats. You are terrific. I know Dad enjoyed his Entenmanns and last night he attacked his fruit snacks. He is just like a little boy. Oh boy, he was delighted to hear me say he can consider both boxes his property. I'll enjoy the wheat wafers.

"What's for dinner tonight?" Oh shucks. Dad says I must not worry so. It is difficult trying to serve a well-balanced meal each day. For myself alone, a portion of meat or fish and rice, potato or macaroni casserole. But Dad needs his vegetables. You know just writing about it now—a "revelation"—with your vegetables, not really too difficult. Thanks for helping me overcome this gigantic daily problem (smile) – a mountain out of a molehill, ceci??

Love you precious—our very own lovely Missy. We are so proud of you. Thanks for choosing us as your parents.

Love, Toots & Dad

Wednesday 11/9/88

Hi darling,

Your Dad has me addressing and mailing [Christmas] *cards already. Adding notes in each makes my hand so very tired after a 2 hour stretch. And to think I am only up to the letter "C." Must remember to add a birthday card for my favorite nephew, Rodney.*

All's well here. Such fun getting your "election" phone call last nite. Your Dad was thrilled to hear from his "baby" but won't write unless I pin him down. No patience to sit quietly to jot a few lines. I'm just the opposite. I'll write and let other things go. We can't all be alike.

The weather is a bit too breezy for me. They call it "Christmas breeze." Everyone else seems to enjoy it—especially Jiggs [Dad's nickname] *on his usual perch—the porch. Both he and Sport* [my cherry head conure parrot] *could have a grand time together.*

This third world country. The mailman did not come out yesterday (Tues) nor today. I phoned the P.O. all day Tues—a busy signal. Hyacinth [one of the housekeepers] *says "they too lazy—they take the phone off the hook." Another try to reach them this morning. Nothing—not even a signal. I phoned the telephone operator to check the number—her report: "Out of order." When I mentioned this to Uncle Jr, he says like any other citizen if they fail to pay "up" their telephone bills, service is cut off. So here I am no wiser—a little burnt up (smile). At least we have one full month. The tix must reach us this week for sure, if not next. Wonder what the mailman's story will be when and if he turns up tomorrow. Your guess is as good as ours.*

I have been meaning to mention—when my letters seem meaningless or pointless, let me know. As if you would (tee-hee).

Oh! I wrote Laurie and family for concern and love during hurricane. So I won't send a Xmas card. Perhaps on yours to the family you can include Toots and Jiggs (please). At least we shall be there so it won't appear too foolish.

Oh! Two families we know (Valerie & fam) and Judith's in-laws are both going to NY for Thanksgiving. I mentioned it to Dad. He thinks perhaps I can come to you Thanksgiving '89 and stay through til Xmas when we can both be with you. Honestly, I don't really know how I would fare leaving him behind. What do you think? No urgency in giving your response—Can hold til we all meet for this Xmas. Speaking of Xmas—"ain't" too far off and I've lost 7-9 lbs. Started cookie binge and right back to where I started. I'm a sad sister!! (agree???) Do hope you find this "missive" readable.

I baked Dad a delicious almond cake using a can of almond paste I picked up at Atlantic Avenue Pathmark.

Oh! We loved the butter parsley noodle packet. Surprising how it puffed right up—enough for a side dish for all three of us. Poor Hyacinth absolutely daft when it comes to expressing appreciation. It was delicious—interesting flavor. Still have another packet—beef flavored—shall enjoy when Hyacinth is off. Thanks again for all these treats.

With undying love,

Toots & Dad

Thanksgiving Nov 24 '88

Hi Precious,

You are that to us, you know. So happy to receive your call this morning at 9 a.m. I had a feeling you would phone early. At least both of us were home.

With Xmas around the corner, you will need help (financially) with the trip to Italy. Just between us—I know how to do it—you need not comment.

Just sent an Xmas card to Mary & Serge and my boys at Baywind (Willem and George). I think I've covered all. And I am happy to report I've completed all my Xmas card addressing. What a job. I can relax until next year. I even remembered Terry Spadaro—I've done well. Amen!!

Dad's at the beach. I've just taken my ham, smothered with your crushed pineapple and mustard—completely cooked—from the oven & a pan of brownies. I can't bake just one item while the oven is lit. That's that.

Hyacinth is fixing brown stew fish and calaloo—still no plaintains. If I had chicken, I would make a bread dressing. I make my own from scratch— very tasty. Oh shucks I could have used your small can of candied sweets. I'll use it Sunday when we have chicken. You may get this after your Italy trip. I know it was marvelous. Excellent company—it is later than we all think. Enjoy.....

Love

Toots & Dad

Affectionately, Toots

Friday 1/7/89

Hi Missy,

Our usual last testament—What a delightful visit—highlighted by our Broadway treat "Les Miserables." You should hear Jiggs describe the thrill. Between us, he really surprised me, fortunately for us. Enclosed is Dad's contribution to telephone bills, etc. My little gift is in the usual place—guess!!

Forget the J.C. Penney dress. My dressmaker will copy.

Love you. So do take care—please please.

Shall ding you when we get in. Dad says please save long distance sheet to give him an idea of charges for Easter.

Toots

Wednesday Jan 11, '89

Hi Missy,

Dad tried 3x to answer your zing last nite and could not get through. I later tried (within 3 minutes) and got through at 7:45 p.m. Thank you so much for the ring.

Beryl much the same—taking in more fluids—still very weak and almost comatose. Dad is there now. I though I would have this ready for the mailman but two telephone calls kept me from finishing this in time. Anyway, Inez usually gives Dad letters to mail so when he goes to the P.O. he will mail this.

Xmas cards are still coming: 6 this morning, 3 yesterday in addition to the stack that was here to greet us.

Not much more to report. I'll leave space for Dad's report on Beryl when he comes in.

Don't forget your fruit cake on the refrigerator door.

Still no beef or mutton. No plantains either. Dad tells me Inez has a small plantain plant that survived the hurricane. So if you do not go to Italy and decide to visit here with friend Keri, we shall have enough to eat. Chicken scarce. Uncle Jr. had two ready for us when we arrived and Dad got 2 more yesterday.

Dad is late returning from Bogue. I am anxious to hear of Beryl.

Love Toots

Hi Baby,

I was out all morning at Bogue, the mechanic and the bank.

Beryl's case is pathetic. I tried to feed her today with glucose and water but she wouldn't swallow any. On Sunday, when the doctor fed her, she took some and had other nourishment—also on Monday but since yesterday she refuses everything. It breaks your heart to see how thin she is and so helpless. We are praying that God will do what is best. Yesterday was her birthday. I know she may not live to pass another. I can't say for sure because she doesn't know one day from another. Inez is bearing up under the strain. All's well otherwise. Went to the beach twice to unwind.

Miss you.

Love Dad

Monday Jan 23 '89

Hi Darling,

Missed your call again this past weekend. Drats. I was serving as sleep-in maid at Bogue Fri—Sat til Sunday 2 p.m. when Dad comes to fetch me.

Home to heat up dinner and serve. If your Dad had any feeling, he'd take me out to dine, considering how tired I came in—up at 4:35 a.m. Inez starts puttering sometimes early. She is quite another story. Sorry darling. I've never lived in poverty and somehow can't take it. What makes it worse—living so cheap—acting so big around her top-top friends—so devoted and hold the Antonios in such "esteem" (my word). And yet no one comes to visit or call while I am there. Seems to me—weekends are when most people are free to be sociable. "Them" too poor for me.

Having dinner 3 p.m., when up drives Vera [Dad's sister-in-law] *from Mandeville. So good to see her even though I was bleary-eyed.*

Fortunately the couple that drove her did not stay. So I heated up curried chicken—mad rice & peas—calaloo. She loved every bit. She brought a huge sack of grapefruits.

Aunt Beryl is still low—but holding on.

Vera is going to Bogue with me Fri at 4 p.m. and will stay overnite til Sat. Then a former maid comes Sat to take over. It's a miracle Inez does not collapse. She goes from 4 a.m. til 6 pm—closes up the house—and in bed by 7 p.m. This is some experience. Miss Inez is a mess.

Vera and I are having a good time together—talking old time stories and so very lovely memories of you as a little girl. And to think the other day I came across two lovely pictures of you "Blondie"—you looked just like a little "Pixie"—cute and adorable.

I am looking forward to our telephone conversation. I started to say "chat" but that sounds too native. With elections just around the corner (Feb 9) the natives are getting jittery. Even Dad has been warned about the streets at night. But church (at nite or anytime) comes first. He refuses to heed. Vera was surprised he left last nite to go to church after a heavy downpour of rain. Can't budge him when he is determined to do his thing. They are all alike.

Inez thinks Dad & Vivian are crazy in their "fanatic" religion and John & Viv think she is the crazy one (smile).

Thank God for our blessings.

Love you Precious. March 20th is not too far away.

Love Toots

Love you Cheri. Longing to see you once again. Hope it won't be too long. God bless you my dear.

Aunt Vera

Tues Jan 24 '89

Hi darling,

Here I am again—thinking all morning of you and anxiously looking forward to my telephone call from you this evening.

Nothing new here. Beautiful weather—not too hot. Dad is able to go to the beach most days.

Don't know if Vera will accompany him to the beach today.

Tomorrow is Wednesday—Bogue day for Dad. Vera will go with him. I shall stay at home to practice (the piano). Hyacinth will be off so we more than likely have leftovers for dinner. It isn't like your Dad to offer to treat for dinner out. Poor soul.

Make the best of each day darling. Please—it is later than we all think. Hurricanes, earthquakes, floods, droughts, train crashes, plane crashes. Enjoy each day darling.

Nothing much to say except don't worry about us. God has been very good to us. Good health—good living—so many blessings. I remember to offer gratitude each day.

Love you Missy. You are our greatest blessing.

Affectionately,

Toots

Sunday 8:30 pm
Oct 8, '89

Hi Missy,

This letter was meant to be shipped into your luggage to thrill you as you travel. However, better late than never. We both thank you, with all that is within for all the lovely treats, even the packet that ended its journey at Customs. C'est la vie! We were deeply touched that you would undertake to travel so much. Thank you is so little. I know you understand the reasonings of the heart.

What a joy to have had you. When Jiggs returned from the airport, I had to say, your visit was akin to a refreshing breeze at springtime. How very thoughtful of you to undergo the hassle with these rude natives. As you can guess, I am quite alone tonight. Thanks for the ding—7:25 Jamaican time. It was good to know you were safely home with Sport. Hope there was not too much damage.

I loved your African ambassador and colonel story. This one you should write in your memoirs. Which leads me to thank you again for the lovely, rich books for my memoirs.

Sorry, when I returned to double-check the room, I failed to notice Marilyn's gift. With my bright self, didn't I have you paged at the airport to check that you had your house keys and to suggest, if time permitted, to check in the shopping area for Pickapeppa. I can just see Marilyn weeping. My fault. I'll certainly get it up to her in December. Not too far off.

Keep well—vitamins—low shoes. The ankle is on the mind—you did not once complain.

Still praying for Locks (Uncle Locksley). *Love to Muskateers.*

Affectionately,

Toots

Mom and Dad at the front gate of the house in MoBay

Monday 9am
Oct 9 '89

Hi darling,

What a gorgeous morning. Still basking in your lovely visit—a real, real treat. A nice break between our visits to N.Y.

You were so relaxed and we had more of you. Promise you can try to do this again between our N.Y. visits.

Violet just came in, smiling in her quiet lady-like manner. I told her you did not realize she would not see you again before the next visit. She really worked all-out to have things ready for you (mango, breadfruits). I am kind of sorry I did not give you two instead of one. And she really went the extra mile. She is really so pleasant. We thank God for her. See—there is always better (in the ocean).

Oh! Sorry about the cold water. I've just learned that Inez is installing a new hot water heater. So sometime this week, I intend to continue my request here for a new one. I've been talking to Dad for years. He mumbles something about cost. So!! What else is new. I must get a new one before January. I keep telling Dad—well not recently—that as I get older, my body won't act too favorably to the cold showers, especially during the cool winter months (Dec Jan Feb). This time I'll put my foot down. He has far too much money on reserve here. May as well as use it up. This will be my project. You see I can be persuasive in my cool way.

Can't help but constantly being concerned re Lock's health.

I know we shall hear from you on this, even before you receive this.

All for now, dear, so that I can have this ready for the mailman when he comes.

Happy reading –

With lots of love for you

Affectionately

Toots & Dad (he is already off to Bogue)

Affectionately, Toots

Sat 8:30 am Oct 14 '89

Hi darling,

Just felt like spending a quiet hour with you before I start the weekend. This is a good practice day and cooking (baking chicken and cake).

Dad goes to the beach. I can't see wasting time in the hot sun.

I have so much fun just going through old (piano) pieces to keep the fingers active. I do very well, considering...

Oh while we are on the subject of music. #1—I know you are dissatisfied with the finish of the grand and you contemplate refinishing some time in the future. #2—you need the space. We have enjoyed the status of a (baby) grand piano since 1938 for me at least and you all your life. So!! I am suggesting selling the grand now. Wally—the piano tuner—will help you with a selling price—nothing under $1000. He had indicated he might want it. Not under $1000. Then between us, we can get a smaller upright. Think it over. Watch new piano ads in the papers. Nothing under $1800 - $1900 for a new one. Give it some consideration. Frankly, I think the timing is good. Between now and Xmas, we can pick up a new one. That's that. Dad sez this is a decision between us. [I replied that it was unthinkable that we should sell that piano—it was a treasured family heirloom—I still have the baby grand. —Cheryl]

Dad is mad at Pauline. She promised to call early in the week and did not. I don't suppose she realized how worried John and Inez were. She (Inez) would collapse (if anything happened to Locksley)—he is her daily bread. My

116

God—I should hate to have to depend on anyone for livelihood, such as I have seen her. Sad sad—no pride—so it is.

Thank God for you, dear. Don't think twice to doing the right thing for peace of mind. We daily thank God for you and your constant generosity.

Have you noticed I am giving serious thought to writing neater? And not as if I am on the run (smile). This is a leisurely visit with you.

Now what else—Sorry I did not insist on you taking that second breadfruit. One whole week later and it is still here. Dad & I shall use it this weekend.

To think you were with us last Sat this time preparing to go to the beach with your Dad.

Dad is still on the porch before going off to the beach.

While practicing yesterday, I came across 2 sheets of paper between music books. So I am using them. Things like these are far too expensive here to throw away (smile). Such a beautiful morning.

I think I covered all I want to say. Except thank you again for the lovely gifts and the two Entenmann pastries. Dad just finished the last of the apple pie last night. I enjoyed a slither (positively the best). Mervin [a close friend of the family from Brooklyn] *used to always rave about Entenmann's apple pie.*

Imagine Dad finally found flour—2 lb. bags at $2.95 each. He grabbed 4 bags—8 lbs. so I am back in business (baking). Now eggs are low and no chickens. They were importing chickens from Georgia and Alabama. They never fully recovered from the hurricane disaster. Now with little foreign U.S. dollars, they had to cut back on imports. Oh well! We can manage. We have *no babies here. Oh! New rate of exchange $6.06. So we buy what we can because prices are going up and up.*

More Sunday –

Good news about Bert [Uncle Jr.'s son]. *He completed all requirements for entry into Police Academy (two years' probation). I must send "Congrats." He must lose 40 lbs. Uncle Jr. just walked in, which reminded me to share the good news with you.*

Dad sez I should attend church. We shall see.

Where did time go? Now Monday 5 p.m. Yesterday I went to church with Dad. He was so protective. Had me sit on the very back pew so I would not get over-heated. A holiday Sunday—"Heroes Day or Heritage Day." The pastor at Miss Hillary's church says the only heritage Jamaicans leave for their children—"reggae and ganja [marijuana]. *"*

Dad's pastor lit into guests in the government—MoBay's mayor and two members of Parliament—asking them to stand up and be counted. Be respectable, honest and resist gifts from drug barons.

Home by 1 p.m. Knocked out. A meager leftover dinner. Off to bed to sleep. I told Dad he was cheap. We could have eaten out. I often wonder why it never occurs to me to order more lobster. Next time.

Love you—miss ya

Toots

Sunday, Oct 29 '89

Hi Missy,

You are unique—and precious to your adoring parents. There are very few who would take the time to share weekend Halloween party and phone the following evening with a full report. This is to assure you, we both more than enjoyed each call with gratitude to God for you. You are a special jewel—and we love and appreciate all your thoughtful gifts of love.

Poor Jiggs is approaching another milestone (73rd birthday). The importance is that he is in excellent health at 70+. I can't gloat because I am not too far behind. Ooops. So we must enjoy each day with love and gratitude.

What a joy—a hot shower in Jamaica. Absolutely extravagant—luxury plus. At least this works—a flip of a switch that lights up and opens 2 pipes. So very simple.

I am not doing too well weight-wise. These cakes. I see what you mean. If it is here, I must taste. We have done without ice cream in the home altogether. What a sacrifice!

And the nerve to invite guests in to dine—no ice cream. We did have Jell-O and cookies.

Dad has his baptismal class performing tonight. A big night for him. He left at 6:45 dressed to kill. I know he will be late tonight.

All for now.

Affectionately, Toots & Dad

Affectionately, Toots

January 16, 1990
First Day of Reggae Sunsplash

Hi darling,

> *Welcome back to Queens from L.A.*

> *Telephone still out of order. Just dead. Thank God the bedroom phone is working.*

> *These Jamaicans can't run anything right. Each time one looks around, something is breaking down (water—electric—telephone). No railway service. Just imagine the only RR service inoperable. Third world mentally and service. As Granny used to say, we are here to "drink the milk—not to count the cows." Smile. You know I often think of her. We did have some fun years together giggling until she commenced to get senile. Oh well—that's life.*

> *Still no word from my printer (completely out of personal stationery).*

> *I owe so many little thank you notes. My trip to Vera went "kaput"—no transportation. Buses are entirely out of the question. Bad reports— crowded—standing room only ½ way to Mandeville, speeding, etc. Not for me.*

> *Vera's letter said, Edna you can come out—like she was doing me the favor. Even Dad sez it sounded so. However, I do save myself extra expenses (transportation –food—and so much work dusting cooking—she has no domestic help). When it comes to cleaning a bathroom—to bend over a tub— as the youngsters say, "Forget it." My Gwendolyn* [one of the housekeepers]

120

has me spoiled rotten. I do nothing—except bake when I wish. She is an excellent cook—nice pleasing manner. Both Dad and I are pleased with her.

I have so much to do—music, sewing and cookies for Dorrell Buddle. And nothing gets done. Junior and I both agree—this heat wave since our return in May makes one lethargic. No energy—sapped out. So I stay indoor quietly—read—go for walks 5 p.m. when it is cooler.

Dad is running so much. Between church crusade at Fletcher's Beach— Bogue and Inez. He is looking so haggard and drawn. I tell him to slow down—and please don't collapse on me (smile). Sept 3 can't come quick enough.

Love you precious
Toots & Dad

Monday, Feb 5 '90

Hi darling,

Here we are again. Another beautiful Monday morning. The mornings here are breathtaking, beautiful, sunny—not too hot. In fact, during the night it was absolutely chilly. I've just written Trevor and Judith sending our love and prayers. I did write rather a nice letter (Dad thinks so). My gift and special talent, so many say. Incidentally, I received a nice letter from Francine's grandmother. She says she sees you occasionally and you are so very pretty with your new hair-do - or is it hair-cut? If you got it, flaunt it.

Your invitation advice to Mary is excellent. Her room is all ready. Any week or weekend, Dad shall happily meet her. Be sure she has our telephone number. It will be nice to have her anytime Feb or March. Just be aware we leave April 10 (for a visit to NY).

Splendid Keri may be coming with you. Anytime do feel free to send any friend down.

Enjoying my current novel "Hold the Dream" by Barbara Taylor Bradford. One criticism—too many characters—far too many. If you are interested, I'll bring it for you. Real thick paperback. Let me know.

This is the usual Monday morning rambling.

Oh! Powell [former pastor of the church Dad attended in MoBay]*—guest speaker for 2 week tent meeting in the country. Preached yesterday a.m. service. Dad is hopping mad. Sez Powell is trying to ease back into Faith*

122

Temple. Oh dear—I'll keep you posted. Dad stayed home last night. So good to have him home. Too mad to attend tent service. Much more fun staying with me (smile). Of course I was in my glory having him home on a Sunday night. If the church doors were open, he would have been there. But the church was closed and everyone was invited to worship at the tent at Tucker St. James. Powell is intent on dividing the church and worst of it, he has some henchmen on the board that keep him posted as to all that goes on. Sad.

Now what else? I baked three loaves French bread—real, real beauties— two pineapple and papaya cakes and 3 dozen cookies for Dorrell Buddle. Today is his birthday. Junior took a nice basket over to him yesterday. He is still so badly crippled with arthritis and barely ambulatory. I should try to visit him later today.

Heard from [Uncle] *Louis this morning. Off again—winter vacation Mexico—Feb 3- March. He just hopes no deaths again while he is on vacation. Both Beryl and Vivian* [one of Dad's older brothers] *died while he and Constance were on vacation.*

Benita's [my cousin] *wedding April 21, 1990 in Vancouver. June 1ˢᵗ— they plan to move from Duncan to a 2-bedroom condo in Victoria.*

All for now

Love, Toots & Dad

May 15, '90

To our darling precious Missy,

What a joy these 30 days have been. One treat after the other. The Williamsburg trip after driving 7 hours turned out to be a long remembered occasion. How do you concoct these precious treats? Happy to see my old friends Bess and Okaleah. Treasured moments.

And the very special highlight of the visit—the mother-daughter luncheon. We mothers are still raving over the day. Frolic, fellowship and fun. A mere thank you seems so very simple—but you must know the sentiment goes deeply to the heart. We are all so very blessed to have such terrific daughters— young women of the 90s. Go to it—enjoy each blessing that comes your way.

May our good Lord and Savior continue to guide your path each day is our heartfelt prayer.

God bless you dear Missy.

Love from Toots & Dad

May 24, 1990

Hi darling,

Welcome home. I am sure you had fun and a gala time. Although Dad read in the papers yesterday that the airport suffered a strike of some kind. To allay his fears, I told him it would not affect you—you were already in Sicily. After checking your itinerary, I discovered you were to leave Greece on the 23rd. Did it affect you? Guess I will know the answer to this on your first telephone call. No—Dad says the strike was the day before your departure.

Each day Dad says I hope my baby is alright. I answer you are a seasoned traveler and shall be very careful. Then you do have a guardian angel that is your constant guide and protector, n'est-ce pas? Of course.

Do hope you remembered Mavis' plate. Just tell her not much time for shopping if you failed to remember. The same applies to my fan.

Just a note darling to say we love you very much. You and your 3 musketeers (Mary, Keri and Marilyn).

Love Toots

Monday May 28 '90

Hi Missy,

Dad has been tracking each day of your journey (Greece Sicily and Amsterdam).

Weather cooled off a bit but hot again today.

I told Uncle Junior I would love to be on the plane to greet you Wed at 138-10.

Hip hip hooray! 231 to 225. Celebrated yesterday with two hefty slices of bun. Back to the diet tomorrow.

My little friend from England (here when I returned) - 45 years old— daughter of the Browns at 8 Tate Street. A real refreshing delight. She leaves for England tomorrow. I shall miss her. We had lots of fun times together. Saved me from missing you too much. No—not at all (smile). When she was not here (while her husband visited his parents in the country parts), I was with her. Since she has to pack, I'll visit her briefly after I complete this.

Just completed dinner—grated cho-cho—looks like cucumber. Makes a delightfully cool and refreshing salad. I had it with chicken salad.

Yesterday—Sunday—I treated Dad to Stove-Top Stuffing with his chicken. I don't think he raved enough considering the box cost $1.59 (smile).

Perspiration just pouring from my head.

Oh—I made a banana cake with my apricot brandy. Looks good. Dad sez it is tasty. He does not know about the brandy. Doreen loved it. I made a loaf for her. So very appreciative. She is the person who gave me the silver coasters I left there. This time, she gave me 4 napkin rings. They may end up in NY. I no longer entertain (dinners) here—far too hot.

Gwendolyn still an excellent maid. $105 for 4 days. She seems very happy and enthusiastic.

All for now darling. Get some rest. One needs a vacation to get over a vacation, n'est-ce pas?

I won't ask Dad to write today. I'll get him for the next letter.

Love you kid

Toots

Tuesday, August 7, '90

Hi Missy.

Here we are again. After all the hoopla. Reggae dance went on until 6 a.m. this morning at Jarrett Park. [In the first few years, the Reggae Sunsplash annual event took place at the park across the street from 17 Tate. It soon outgrew the park and moved to a permanent facility in Freeport]. *I phoned the police at 3 a.m to ask that they send an officer to the site to have them lower the mike. They did but by 5 a.m. it was louder than ever. Oh well. These Jamaicans have no regard for others.*

Always such a thrill talking with you. Each call brings its own thrills. Thanks dear. Life would be so dull here without your refreshing calls— honestly.

Since Dad has been home more, life is again hunky-dory—as I like it. He just came in from the beach with a large bottle of Anais Anais perfume for me. Well—this is more like it. I think they all need jacking up once in a while. No one takes Toots for granted. I'll show him.

Oh dear I've not yet written Willem and George. Do hope George continues to get well. We shall miss them when they move—I know you will. Nothing exciting to report.

Toots is happy again. Hooray! Oh don't forget to upgrade our Xmas trip Dec 17—Jan 18. Dad is happy he can make the Xmas party.

Love Toots

April 6, 1995

Hi Honey

"Tempus Fugit"

Very soon we will be there. Looking forward to a few weeks of fun with you. Do hope the weather will treat us favorably.

See you soon.

Love Dad

Oct 9, '95

Dearest Missy,

What a delightful telephone call we enjoyed with you on our 51ˢᵗ [wedding anniversary]. Can't believe another year has gone by so quickly. I really do feel one year younger.

This morning, after all week's heavy torrential rains—a beautiful sunny morning.

I feel younger than springtime. Hooray—thank God.

Dad went to the airport (with Junior) to pick up our Tampa tickets Dec 12—Jan 11. I am ready to go now. Except I need to see a definite buyer (for the house on Tate Street). Two good possibilities so far.

Believe it or not, we are still in hurricane season. Dad and Junior went to the beach and found the seas too high for safe swimming. They went for a walk and came home 1 hour earlier.

Yes—when I say we (your Dad and I) are still like two kids—believe it if you can. But this morning—5 a.m. before he left for the beach, he made the same observation "We are like two kids." Take it as the gospel truth.

All for now.

Love from Toots & Dad

*Dad had to drag Mom to the beach and when
she got there she had a great time.
Here they are, clowning at Fletcher's Beach in Montego Bay*

March 3, 1996

Darling

Just a lovely note to say Congratulations on achieving an outstanding "A" on your recent math course [statistics class for my master's degree]. *Let's hope the worst is behind you. Hooray—you really suffered.*

Up to our neck packing—to ship 2 barrels—2 old trunks and 4 suitcases to travel with us. We expected shippers in 2/29 to give an estimate of cost. Not a word. These people are so unreliable. Made another appointment for Thurs 3/7. We plan to ship late so we shall be there to receive everything. I also have 2 small boxes of books. I've had to give away most of my (dear friends) books. No room in the Inn for more books.

I tell my young friends to make believe they are moving every 5 years to weed out unwanted items.

You do make us very proud. Thanks.

With all our love—until 1ˢᵗ or 2ⁿᵈ week in April. "Deos volente."

Affectionately,

Toots & Dad

50th Wedding Anniversary

My mother was fearless. The only time I can recall seeing her frightened was the prospect of not living long enough to see her 50th wedding anniversary. I don't know why it was so important to her, but it seemed to represent some sort of finish line, as if marking a victory in a race. She often lamented over friends who had been married and one of the spouses had died before they reached that milestone. In her mind, the tragedy was not that the spouse had died, but that she or he hadn't lived to celebrate their Golden anniversary.

Fortunately, her fears proved to be unfounded. My parents celebrated their 50th anniversary on October 7, 1994, while living in Jamaica. They rented a cottage for three days at Half Moon Resort in Montego Bay. At the time, I was living in Amsterdam. Thanks to generous Dutch work regulations, employees got three days time off to celebrate their parents' 50th anniversary. So I flew to New York, spent the night, and caught a flight the next morning to MoBay. I had called Mom and Dad from New York, but led them to believe I was still in Holland. I was flying stand-by on an airline employee's discount ticket, so I wasn't sure I would make the flights. I didn't tell my parents I was coming—I didn't want them to be disappointed if I didn't make it.

I did call the hotel to let them know of my surprise visit, though. When I arrived, the hotel staff whisked me to the cottage in a golf cart. I was giddy with excitement as I burst into the room and yelled "Surprise! Happy Anniversary!" I saw Dad's eyes light up and he greeted me with his usual "Hey, baby." But to my amazement, Toots just looked at me and said "I knew you were coming" and then she just kept talking as if I'd been there for days instead of minutes. I could never surprise her!

We shared a wonderful day together. The weather was great, the resort was beautiful and we laughed like "three bugs in a rug," as Toots used to say.

Three bugs in a rug. Me, Toots and Dad at Half Moon Bay

I had bought them a gift from a silversmith in Holland that had cost a small fortune in guilders. It was a picture frame and stand that was engraved with their names, the date and the words "Happy Anniversary." The hotel staff brought beautiful flowers to the cottage and sent a photographer to take pictures. One of my favorite pictures is the three of us wearing sunglasses—I called it our Blues Brothers picture, even though my parents had no idea who the Blues Brothers were.

That evening, we got dressed up—Mom in a gold blouse and long black skirt, Dad in his tuxedo—and had dinner at the hotel's outdoor restaurant overlooking the beach. During dinner, the manager made an announcement of their anniversary and everyone clapped; people came over to extend their congratulations. Mom and I used to call Dad "Mr. Mayor" because he loved to talk to strangers, and very soon, his jacket came off and he was making the rounds of all the tables, making new friends. A huge cake came out after dinner and we shared it with everyone in the restaurant. It was such a relaxing evening, outdoors under the stars, listening to the waves crashing on the beach. Whenever I think of Jamaica, I hear those waves. Even now, when I go to any beach, I don't care if I go in the water. As long as I can hear the waves, I'm happy.

After dinner, we went into a grand room with a huge chandelier and a baby grand piano. It was probably the first baby grand piano my mother had seen since living in Jamaica, and she sat down and began to play. Another great photo op.

The next morning, we had breakfast and spent the rest of our time together doing what we always did best—talking. That afternoon, I took a flight back to New York and then home to Amsterdam. On the long flight home, I remember an overwhelming sense of relief—I knew my mother was happy now that she and Dad had lived to celebrate this wonderful occasion together.

Dad and Mom, at piano, in library at Half Moon, after dinner.
50th anniversary celebration

Looking back, I wonder why I never asked her why that anniversary was so important. Although we talked a lot, most times it was more along the lines of "idle chatter." My mother was not emotional and I can't recall any really serious, deep conversations with her. We would talk about "things" but not the "whys," not the underlying feelings. Sometimes I got the impression that any show of emotion was a sign of weakness; sometimes I thought she just never wanted to deal with anything negative. I can remember many times when I just thought to myself: I'll ask her later. Of course, later never came. I always thought there'd be time for explanations someday. The family tree would be complete: I'd know all about all of her friends, childhood and present; I'd understand how she viewed her life, her husband, her children. That day never came. Lots of questions are unanswered. The more I think, the less I know. Toots was an enigma, a woman of many layers, not at all transparent. Her mind worked as fast as her fingers could fly across a keyboard. She would start one subject, ask one question, and while you were still thinking of an answer, she was already on another topic. I always got the feeling that I was a few steps behind her. Toots was larger than life— formidable, I think is the word. No one would challenge her. I feared I could never walk in her footsteps. Never mind that I was supposed to be my own person—I wanted to be just like her. I wanted to be strong, not easily swayed, my mind always clearly made up, always sure of myself, no match for any challengers. Many things are clearer in retrospect, but some parts of my mother's essence will always be a mystery to me.

The Journal: 1999—2000

1999: Dad beginning to change in behavior. Remembering less and less. Hearing becoming impaired. Incidentally, Cher and I advised to have a hearing test. Of course, he was against this. "Nothing is wrong with my hearing." Cheryl and I decided if I had a representative of the hearing company pay a house visit for my testing, we somehow could break down Dad's defenses. Results—my hearing is good. And yes—we succeeded in having Dad's hearing checked. Results—he is losing 60% of what is said and hearing only 40-45%. This is not moving Dad. He decided the agent was just out to make a sale for a hearing device. The end of this episode.

2000: Hearing loss more so evident. In addition to problems of the aging, he is now 85. I try to reason with him gently, that we are both aging together. "No" he says, "I am as young as I ever was. Whatever I did 20 years ago I can still do." My reply: "Excellent."

His hearing is pronouncedly declining. He still stubbornly announces that he can hear what he wants to hear. I was shocked. How very sad. I am beginning to fear we are losing the beautiful love we always shared. And I must realize these acts and statements are signs of the aging.

I often question my own behavior and definitely realize I am not as vibrant as I once was. There are definite limitations one must come to grips with and accept them. This morning, Friday, I awoke with a headache. I told

Dad I would like to have the day off from kitchen duty. I had enough food leftover, provided that Dad need only heat up. He said OK.

Saturday, I awakened with the same headache. Thought I'd spend the morning discarding papers and catalogs. There's never an end to the catalogs and papers. This morning, I decided to bite the bullet again. When Dad came into the bedroom and saw me surrounded by papers, books, etc. all I got was an old man's grunt. So I announced, rather than asked, "Would you have enough dinner for today's meal" I was somewhat baffled by his reply. "I always take care of myself—why ask now?" I was mortified. After 57 years of service, this is evidence how quickly we can forget service of the past.

The Journal: 2000

Age 80. One day I suggested to my John that I'd like to plan to give at least one more piano recital. I expected a comment. No comment—not even a murmur.

I've enjoyed each day—doing what I like—when I like—how I like. This has been an enjoyable year with a devoted John of 56 years. Cheryl honored the year with a gala birthday party. I had such fun with old schoolmates. I feel vibrant.

In June, I finally wrote a letter to my estranged brother:

Hi there.

In this life, we are fortunate and free to choose our friends. With choice of family, we are not so endowed. It remains up to each individual to adjust to each member, however diverse, and maintain a harmonious relationship. And so on the eve of entering a new decade—as a vibrant, ecstatic and loving 80 year older—I take this opportunity to apologize for any unknown element of discord and offer prayers for a more fruitful relationship.

Sincerely,

ECA

Cheryl Elferis

Some thoughts:

Life is like a bubble
Two things stand like stone
Kindness in another's trouble
Courage in our own.

Patterns of life: one thing prepares one for the other.

Tomorrow one must do things you think you cannot do today.
Surround yourself with people who are positive and godly.
My home should be an oasis of dignity, hospitality and civility.

Friends and Family

Mom never received a reply to the letter she sent to her brother [Uncle Junior]—not even a phone call. Why they were estranged was a mystery to me, as well as to her. She could not fathom why her brother scorned her repeated attempts for reconciliation, or even why he was angry with her. However, Toots often said, "Blood is not thicker than water." I always took this to mean that relatives could not always be counted upon and that sometimes just because you were related, that didn't mean that there was any real bond between you. Conversely, you could have stronger ties with the friends you chose. She never worried about me being an only child or being alone because she realized that while I didn't have sisters or brothers, I had friends who would be there for me, no matter what.

Toots truly had perfected the art of making lifelong friends out of casual acquaintances. After God, relationships were the most important thing in one's life. She kept in touch with almost all of her childhood schoolmates. At her funeral, I couldn't believe how many had said they had gone to school with her or lived in the same neighborhood when they were children.

Putting this journal together gave me the wonderful opportunity to reminisce with some of Mommy's childhood friends. Some I keep in touch with on a regular basis; others I hadn't seen since I was a child. The best stories came from the Girls of Greene Avenue—all grew up on the same block as Toots.

There's Betty Fletcher, now aged 87, still living in the same house on Greene Avenue that she moved to at age 11, in 1927. During our interview, she threatened to sue me if I didn't say nice things about her. But I have only fond memories of Betty—her nephew, Avery, went to public school with me and was one of my best friends. She refreshed my memory on long-forgotten names of neighbors on our block. Her best childhood memory is that my mother used to come by to borrow her ice skates. Betty never wanted to lend them to my mother, but apparently even when Betty wasn't there, her father would lend them out. Seems Betty never used the skates. The girls didn't go to school together, they only knew each other as neighbors, but always kept in touch throughout the years.

Wherever I traveled, Mom would ask me to bring back the foreign stamps; she was giving them to Betty, who was an avid collector. Betty was one of the very few people who always sent my dad cards after Mommy passed away, and it always brought a huge smile to his face when he saw her return address. I think it was because of those cards that Betty was one of the few people Dad remembered until he went into the nursing home. For that simple act of kindness, I will always be grateful to Betty.

Marilyn, now 84, lived at 300 Greene Avenue, next door to the Craigs. She recalls their parents talking to each other over the backyard fence. She was a few years younger than Mom. Eventually, she moved to Manhattan and married and the two lost touch. One day, she went the to 3rd Avenue Y, and saw the nameplate: Edna Craig Antonio. In Marilyn's words: "What a thrill! We hugged and kissed!" Then, they lost touch for a few more years. In 1983,

Marilyn received a phone call from a woman saying she was a "voice from the past." The voice was Toots. The two women renewed their friendship. I often heard them on the phone, whispering and giggling like two teenage girls. In her last years, especially when she was in pain, I remembered thinking how great it was that she had a special friend like Marilyn.

I had the most delightful conversation with Harriette, who grew up on the second floor in Betty's house. Although 81, she had the heartiest laugh; she was so happy to hear from me, she must have said "Oh Jesus" at least a hundred times. Her mother died when she was 14 and Paubee and Granny took the responsibility of raising her. She and Mom both went to Mrs. Borland's Dance School on Monroe Street and Classon Avenue, and always kept in touch. Her words of wisdom: "It's a bitch to get old!"

In 1936, at Dr. McCoy's house on Greene Avenue, my mother met Vivian and Frank. My mother, then 16, played the piano at Dr. McCoy's Friday night prayer meeting. For Vivian and Frank, the weekly prayer meetings served as their Friday night date. The three quickly became friends and double-dated after John came to New York. Eventually, John, Frank and Vivian attended the same church and continued their life-long friendship. They were all active in ministry and when I was 13, "Sister Hock" was my Sunday School teacher. And for many years, I had the privilege of working with their daughter Caryl in one of the children's ministry programs. We are good friends to this day, always swapping travel stories.

Eileen, also an accomplished pianist, was another good friend of Mom's. They met at Siloam Presbyterian Church when Eileen was 17. By sheer coincidence, also at the time, Eileen was taking piano lessons from a woman who lived on the top floor of Mommy's house at 298 Greene. After they married, Eileen and Mom lost touch for several years, until my parents moved back to Queens in 1996.

Mazie remembers my mother's encouraging spirit. When she was her 10, Mom was her piano teacher. Mazie's parents knew the Craigs from Jamaica. Mazie recalls performing a duet in a concert with another student. She was extremely nervous—she wanted to be a singer, not a piano player—but Mom encouraged her to play and to do well. When Mom came back from Westwood, Mazie says all she talked about was the wonderful man she had met and how much she was in love. Even though Mazie moved to Las Vegas, they always kept in touch.

Sylvia worked with Mazie at the telephone company for many years. Ironically, Sylvia already knew my mother through her cousin, Mervin who lived in the same neighborhood. Sylvia remembers my dad giving her a ride home after a party at Mervin's house. Mervin's wife, Doris, was one of my godmothers. No one seems to know how the friendship between Mervin and my parents started, though. They had three sons- one my sister's age, one my age, and one slightly younger. Growing up, we spent a lot of time at each other's homes and were great childhood friends.

Marilyn S. met Mommy through mutual friends in the old neighborhood, Dorothy and her sister, Jeri. Mom had gone over to say good-bye the week before she and Dad retired to Jamaica. She remembers Toots saying, "Don't get old—you'll fall apart in pieces."

"Aunt" Mavis met my parents when she first came to New York in November 1948. She had been given their phone number by mutual friends in Jamaica. Upon arrival, Mavis called my parents to introduce herself and she recalls that they were anxious to meet her. She was staying with an aunt of hers, but on weekends, she escaped to spend time at the house on Greene Avenue. My uncles Louis and Locksley were also living at Greene Avenue at the time (both were in medical school) and they all played bridge together.

Mavis' recollections of Mom: "She got involved in everybody's lives. When she cooked, she didn't just cook for her immediate family—she cooked for everybody." Aunt Mavis became my godmother, and on the day of my sister Jean's funeral, she was the one who stayed home with me while everyone else went to the church.

Rodney ("RaRa") and Arnold are my two closest cousins. To them and everyone else in the family, Toots was "Auntie." Rodney grew up in the house with me on Greene Avenue until he was about 14 years old, then he went to live with his mother on Macon. His recollections: "Auntie was really cool. She took us to places that average kids didn't go to, like concerts. I recall one occasion when I was 13, and I came home with a pack of cigarettes in my pocket. I went upstairs to the third floor for an afternoon snack. Auntie made the best tuna fish sandwiches; she cut the crusts off and made them with pickle relish. Much to my chagrin, Uncle Johnny saw the cigarettes and said, 'Oh, now you think you're a big man.'

"At one concert, during intermission, everyone went outside. She smoked non-filtered Kools and she offered me a cigarette. I felt like a grown person. It was a great feeling. She never smoked in front of Uncle Johnny. Once in a while, she would sneak a cigarette in the bathroom.

"Once, she slapped me when I was being a smart aleck. Auntie had asked me 'What do you love?' I mumbled something and then she asked me, 'Who do you love?' I said, 'Myself,' and the next thing I knew, I saw stars."

*Toots and Rodney, 1947, taken across the street
from our home on Greene Avenue, Brooklyn*

Arnold lived on Macon Street with his mother, Aunt Gloria. "Auntie was very opinionated, as all mothers are. She always looked out for me and always reminded me of my manners. As a child, I didn't appreciate that but in reality, it was a benefit. When I was an adult, I would call her up and ask her for recipes. My favorites were rice and peas, baked ziti and cookies. I still have the original recipes in her handwriting. For Christmas and birthdays, I always got beautiful cards with nice narratives in them. Whenever I needed to talk to someone, I would phone Auntie. In reality, she was like a foster mother to me."

There are so many more names in my mother's phone book that could attest to their lifetime of friendship.

If I remember anything my mother ever said, it is this: "The men in your life will come and go, but your women friends will always be there for you." Boy, was she right. Girlfriends I met when I was 10 and in my 20s and 30s are closer than sisters to me. I imagine those friendships will continue forever. How many hours have we spent on the telephone or over meals in not-so-fancy restaurants? An unkind word or angry moment has never passed between us. Time spent with girlfriends is like staring into a mirror; it is through them that you really come to know yourself.

Toots never understood women whose lives revolve exclusively around the men in their lives—women who neglect their girlfriends whenever a new romantic interest comes along; women who only call their girlfriends when they need help or advice; women who have never traveled anywhere with their girlfriends. I don't understand them either.

Friends who came with me to visit my parents after they retired to Montego Bay quickly learned how to "assume the position" on the porch and do absolutely nothing but watch the world go by. A sign of true friendship is being in each other's company and not having to say a single word.

The Journal: 2001

Age 81. This year passed so quickly without incident. Gradually growing old. I see definite changes in activities due to less energy. We do, however, try to eke out any happiness we can. I take joy in thrilling so many shut-ins and elderly friends with letters, notes and love.

My mind works like lightning. One brilliant flash and it's gone!

11/15/01: Important to share with Dr. Blum and Cheryl

a) *Premonition: 5 am. During a dream, I reached over to pat John and realized the person in bed with me was not John but my mother. Of course, I was stunned. Then later, I went to the living room and there was my dad waiting for me. This puzzled me. I remained quietly reflecting. Then my tummy swelled up hard. I remembered I had no formal meal—just tomato and seltzer water. Oh my God—could this be the end? I got up and took a large dose of Mylanta. Then stayed up to write memoirs for CCE.*

b) *Last night while John was out at prayer meeting. I'd just watched Jeopardy and Wheel. The telephone rang—I got up quickly and moved cautiously to the phone, when the room began to spin. Ooops. I can't afford to fall now. The doors are locked and I am totally alone. I took my time getting to the phone, but that was scary.*

Some thoughts:

Good friends are presents from God.
Age is mind over matter. If you do not mind, what does it matter?
Love is the highest work we can accomplish.
Every couple has it's own raison d'etre.
Every ending is a new beginning.

Small minds discuss people.
Average minds discuss events.
Great minds discuss ideas.

Treat people with respect. Love the God within them.
I put a great deal of emphasis on positive affirmation. It is my mental fertilizer.

The Journal: 2002

February 2002: Valentine's Day. Not even a kiss from him. Of course no gift. All our married life, John considered this day as a gimmick for shoppers and manufacturers. Cheryl and Gary gave me a huge heart-shaped cookie inscribed Happy Valentine's Day. I gave Dad a can of Danish butter cookies. I started to say his favorite, but he has no favorite anything.

Toots and Gary

Last night, we turned in to bed early; he dozed off at 8 pm. I stayed up and listened to the TV in the bedroom, so he won't accuse me of staying in the living room and avoiding him. His selfish streak is rearing its ugly head. When he awakened at 9:30 pm, he reached for my hand for an embrace. Oh! Oh! What's next? I reminded him to please not wake me early the next morning. He awakened quietly enough at 4:30 am as usual for devotions in the living room. But at 7:30, getting back into bed, he made so much noise that he woke me anyway. I pretended to be asleep, but I was fit to be tied. After begging last night, oh shucks, I can't win. At 10:15 am, I finally got up to make a carrot cake. After the cake went into the oven, I sat down to enjoy my coffee—still warm, but I turned it into iced coffee. Cleo [my beagle that I used to bring over every morning to spend the day with Toots] *arrived. 11:00 am—Dad started to fidget, preparing to "steam up for dinner." I remind him—How different we were from each other. I jump out of bed to bake for friends. He is ready to be served. I said "Dad, everything is ready. You just heat up everything for your dinner. Can you manage?" "I'll survive" says he, implying he gets no service anyway. He is getting so so bitter. How very very sad. I am appalled my Honey should take this attitude.*

I just could not let the sun go down without clearing the air. Prepare yourself—it gets worse. No solutions. Lots of prayer goes up for patience. He does not realize the change in his attitude—the approach of senility.

I asked sincerely "Do you think we are drifting apart?" No common ground here, no matter how I try. Leave it to God in prayer. I went on to say "Dad, you have known all our 57 years together that you are always first in my life." "Not so," said he, "you are always pushing me away." No response. This is the sign of a selfish man. He cannot reason now when there is nothing to discuss or reason on his side. Do I give up? No. No. No. Keep seeking a solution to regain what we once had—a beautiful romance. There are always changes in growth.

Age 82. Definitely no longer a vibrant lady. Growing old is definitely no fun.

Longfellow:

   Tell me not, in mournful numbers

   Life is but an empty dream

   For the Soul is dead that slumbers,

   And things are not what they seem,

   Life is real, Life is earnest,

   And the grave is not its goal;

   Dust thou art, to dust returnest

   Was not spoken of the soul.

Tennyson:

   Ah, sad and strange as in dark summer dawns

   The earliest pipe, when into dying eyes

   The casement slowly grows a glimmering square

   So sad, so strange, the days that are no more.

The Antonios: By wisdom is a house built, and through understanding it is established. Through knowledge its rooms are filled with rare and beautiful treasures. Proverbs 24: 3,4.

Affectionately, Toots

Trust in the Lord with all your heart and lean not on your own understanding. In all your ways acknowledge Him and he will direct your paths. Proverbs 3: 5,6.

Cheryl: My Dreams

Since 2003, I've had two very vivid dreams about Toots.

In the first, I dreamt that my mother came back from the dead. She was healthy and walking around as if there had never been anything wrong with her legs. The first thing I said to her was that I had already given all her jewelry away. I thought she would be mad but she just said that was okay and smiled. Then I thought to myself: I still have to tell her I gave all her clothes away to the Salvation Army and that Gary and I had moved into her bedroom. Then I wondered how many more years we would have together before she died again.

In the second dream, I died and went to heaven. I saw Jesus and the only thing he said was "Go find your family." The first person I saw was Gary. He said "Hi Cheryl—I'm talking to a friend I used to work with in Florida." He was standing in front of a house with a narrow, winding staircase and he said my parents were upstairs and I should go see them. I climbed to the top of the staircase and there was a large room with a gable roof. My parents were resting on a bed by the window. They said "Hi" like we had been together forever and didn't seem surprised to see me. I said, "What do you do here?" And Dad replied, "You can do whatever you want. We're just waiting." I looked out the window and saw a big field with lions walking around and children were playing. My mother asked me if I could pick out my sister Jean.

I saw one girl with long black hair but Dad said no—that wasn't her. I pointed to another girl about 5 years old—she had long bushy hair and a plaid jumper. And Mom told me yes that was Jean—why don't you go say hello to her? So I went down the narrow staircase and out to the field. I went up to Jean and said "Hello I'm your sister Cheryl." And she answered, "Yes, I know. I'm playing with my friends. Do you want to play?" And I just looked around and was amazed that the lions were walking around in the midst of the children playing. And then I woke up.

Mothers and Daughters, Continued

Since I didn't have sisters, my mother became my confidante. I told her everything. Absolutely nothing fazed her. I never saw her emotionally unsettled or shaken by any circumstance. It was really hard to ruffle her feathers. She has to have been one of the most even-tempered people I have ever known.

Only twice can I recall seeing her cry. Once was after she had gotten off the phone with her sister. Although obviously distraught, she refused to say what was upsetting her. Not until many years later did I find out about the discord between Mom and her siblings.

I never heard her raise her voice at anyone, although she was not the most patient person. On the other hand, very little really excited her (other than the sound of the Mister Softee ice cream truck).

Affectionately, Toots

Toots and me, sitting outside a friend's house in the Catskills.
Summer 1988

158

The Elderly

Mom always had a soft spot for the elderly. I can remember, as a child, taking the bus on Gates Avenue to visit blind Mr. Coakley in a nursing home. We visited others too, but I don't remember their names. I don't even know what Mr. Coakley's relationship to our family was. All I know is there is a $10 gold coin on a chain in our safe deposit box that he gave my mother. It was probably the only thing of value he ever owned. One day, we stopped going to the nursing home. I remember asking her why we weren't going there anymore. She just replied that we didn't need to go anymore. I guess that was her way of telling me Mr. Coakley had passed away, but I don't think I understood that until many years later.

Homebound

In 1999, a relapse of Guillain Barre syndrome greatly reduced her mobility. She became fearful of walking outside, worrying that she would fall and not be able to get up. It didn't help that Dad, with his progressing Alzheimer's, became increasingly unhelpful. He refused to push Mom in a wheelchair, even though that would have allayed her fears about falling. If she fell in the street, he was just going to leave her there. Rather than risking an injury and not being able to rely on Dad, Toots became more and more confined to home. However, she didn't let that stop her.

Moving from the bed to the recliner in the living room became her longest walk. But she found a new area of ministry—encouraging others, by phone and by mail. Anyone in a nursing home or hospital got a phone call almost every day. Everyone else got a handwritten note or card. She made it a point to write at least 10 letters a day and she wouldn't stop until she had reached her quota. When I lived in Amsterdam, there was a letter from her every single day in my mailbox. Living in a foreign land with friends and family far away, those letters from home were my lifeline, even if she only talked about the meatloaf she had made the night before.

I found her list of birthdays and anniversaries—it had more than 200 names on it, including those of my friends. She always reminded me of my friends' special occasions. Since she hasn't been around, I have been terribly remiss in remembering those occasions. I do still write as many notes as I can—to her friends, my friends, and former students.

Mom in the chair in which she wrote most of her letters.
This photo was taken in 1997

While cleaning out the apartment after her death, I found what seemed like every card and every note anyone had ever sent her. Gary and I estimate that we threw away half a ton of paper. Yet, I know that she wrote probably twice or three times as much as she received. Dad used to joke that it cost him more to keep her supplied in stationery and postage than it did to clothe and feed her.

In one large box, I found about a hundred identically handwritten notes in envelopes, some addressed and stamped, some not. Toots must have written the letters sometime shortly after she was released from the hospital in December 2002. It seems she had written a "master copy" and was copying it to send to all of her friends. In essence, she was saying farewell. It was indeed, in very shaky handwriting, the last letter.

The Last Letter

Dear dear friend,

For the past two years, I've been living in a "fool's paradise" thinking that in the octogenarian years I could continue to enjoy life as I've always known.

Suddenly, mid-year 2002, it began to dawn on me: "The golden years are not so golden." Ooops, I suddenly realized—life could never be the same.

New limitations being imposed on what strength was available was a real shock. Nevertheless, I paused quietly to give God all the (indecipherable) gratitude provided for good long-term Christian praying friends.

And so it goes—until December 9th a sudden twist in life occurred. Guillain Barre Syndrome once again curtailed all physical movement from the waist down. I collapsed and was hospitalized for 9 days. Crying into the night, and by day begging for permission to return home to care for John (86). His latest medical procedure revealed additional memory loss. Of course, he is in denial (so what else is new?). He says I have the problem. Excellent, says I.

So here we are. Two former lovebirds for 58 years, no longer able to cope.

Thank you for your friendship, your prayers and your love. Here's to better days ahead.

Affectionately, Toots

I am a firm believer. One's mind governs the body—given the chance.

Pray, friends, dear dear Christian friends.

Edna

In the End

In the last year, Mom became increasingly demanding and sometimes cranky. She wasn't given to complaining and it was unlike her to dwell on her infirmities. Her letters to friends in the last few months revealed her lack of will to go on. She was fighting for every ounce of energy and the struggle was just too much. She could not accept her fading abilities. Her mind was sharp but her body would not cooperate.

Dad's declining mental capacity didn't help. We knew there was something wrong long before he was officially diagnosed with Alzheimer's. Now, not only could he not take of her, he couldn't even take care of himself. The man she had spent 58 years of her life with had disappeared. "Her John" was no longer there. It seemed to be truly the only circumstance in her life that she could not deal with.

She left the earth the same way she had lived her life—no fuss, no fanfare. I never heard her say "I wish I had done so-and-so in my lifetime." How fortunate to have no regrets—to have achieved every goal—to feel truly blessed—to sleep peacefully every night. If Toots did it, so can we.

In the end, we are left with memories, too often quickly fading. I sometimes can't remember her voice or recall her touch. I look at pictures of trips but can't remember what we laughed about. I sniff her empty perfume bottles but the scent seems strange, disconnected. I look at her sheet music -

boxes and boxes of it. The notes look familiar and I can picture her fingers flying over the keyboard, but I can't hear the melody.

What I would like to forget are the details of February 20th, 2003: The sudden rush of anger I felt when Gary told me she had died, at home, of a stroke. The ticking of the meter in the taxicab on the ride home. The heaviness of the silence in the empty house. The heat of the sun on my face even though it was winter. The footsteps in the hospital hallway. The uncomfortable look on the doctor's face when she came to "console" us in the family room. Worse yet, the look of unbelief on Dad's face when he finally understood his partner of 58 years was gone. We had no time to grieve - only thoughts of how on earth are we going to take care of Dad. The mind, kicking into high gear, planning, organizing, coping.

Years later, I am no longer distressed over the things I cannot remember. Her dying has taught me how to live. In death, the words she spoke all her life acquired a new and fresh meaning. Live each day to the fullest. Have no regrets. Enjoy every moment. Treat your spouse like you are still on your first date. Cherish true friendships. Be at peace.

I had almost written, "all" we are left with is memories. But I realize we are left with much more. We are left with hope: A hope that we still have time to fulfill our dreams and realize our destinies. A hope that we can learn from the lives which have impacted us in a positive way. A hope that we, in turn, will leave a legacy that will be cherished and remembered by many. Most of all, a hope that we will see our all our loved ones again. It is this hope that sustains and even empowers us to reach beyond the impact of the death of a loved one.

I have this hope.

Six years after her passing, I no longer think of my mother in terms of her death, but rather what she accomplished during her wonderful life. Not only for herself, but for the many lives she impacted with her actions and words of encouragement. Traveling down this road of remembrances, I learned as much about myself as I did about Mom and her family.

I still miss her terribly. But I keep in touch with many of her girlfriends, now all in their 80s and 90s themselves. Even though when I telephone them, I still identify myself as "Cheryl, Edna's daughter."

But most of all, I can now say her name. And to Edna Louise Craig Antonio, I say "Yes I will—I will meet you there."